DEAR AMERICA

DEAR AMERICA

REFLECTIONS ON RACE

EDITED BY NICOLE MATHEW, AMBER PECKHAM, JESSICA DYER, BRAD KING, & ELISE LOCKWOOD

The Geeky Press

Indianapolis, IN

Contents

Poetry

Scripts

Introduction

We are proud to bring you *Dear America: Reflections on Race*.

This is our first anthology in the Dear America series, one we'll expand in the future to tackle other topics of national interest. Before you read the fantastic writers in this anthology, we thought it important to tell you how this collection came together.

We launched The Geeky Press in Indianapolis with the intention of creating platforms for writers to tell their stories. One of the ways we've done that is through several anthology series. Our first, *Bad Jobs & Bullshit*, was a collection of funny stories about terrible, hilarious, bullshit work experiences.

We loved that project (and we'll continue it soon), but it left us longing for something more. We wanted our next project to give writers a chance to tell stories about a topic that mattered, now, right now, to one of our most critical national conversations.

That's when it hit us: We wanted to do an anthology about race.

We had several discussions about how we should approach the project before we announced it. Race isn't an easy topic. In the United States, it comes with a long and violent history and present. And while we believed it was important to build this platform for writers to tell their stories, we also wondered if five white editors should be the folks in charge of the project.

We talked about it quite a bit, both internally and externally. In the end, we decided that we should do the project and that it was — in some way — our responsibility to create this platform and then let the writers do what they do best. The only restriction we put on the stories was that they not be manifestos. We weren't (and aren't) interested in telling people how to think.

And while we believe in free speech and the right to say what you want, we also reserved the right to edit our collection in a way that represented the values we have as a collective. We expressed those in two ways: We tried to be as inclusive as we could in getting our call outside our immediate circles, and we weeded out stories we felt were racist. Not interested. We wanted this platform to be a safe place where people can celebrate stories different from their own.

Despite our good intentions, we still faced a few questions about the project. People were rightfully wary of our goal and our process. And those questions prompted us to have conversations about race, privilege, and our role in the larger conversation happening in the country. We're glad we had them even when they were difficult to have.

That said, more than one hundred writers from across the world submitted their work. We received so many that we had to shut down the call two months early. We knew the anthology's acceptance would depend upon the strength of the writers. Ultimately, our readers will determine if we accomplished our goals, but as the editors, we can say that the stories we were trusted with humbled us.

We hope each of these pieces sparks something in you, as they did in us.

Essays + Creative Nonfiction

Returning Home to America Through the Prophet Poet Langston Hughes

Samuel Son

"Go back home Chink!"

Someone pissed black ink all over the front door and wall of our house.

We moved in only two weeks before.

Graffiti is homo sapiens' territory marking; in this case, a creative expression degraded to dog's piss, a prophetic art blemished to a slur, a spray of angry expulsion: "Get the fuck outta here!"

After six years of roach-infested, intermittent heating apartment, this was our first house, a step towards the American dream, a small plot of earth to our name, with a yard for us to tend, fenced by steel mesh, though not white-pickets a fence nevertheless. We turned this Long Island 70's ranch house into our home. Grandmother taped up grainy black &white photos of her husband gone now for two years; my two brothers and I put up Met's 86 World Champions poster featuring Jesse Orosco's lovers jump to his catcher in our bedroom; living room was done in the poor man's interior design, i.e. any hand me down furniture that fit into our church van, arranged physically, not aesthetically. The final signature was the kitchen. It took only one weekend for our kitchen to reflect mother's culinary chaos — cooking for anyone ringing our bell with ingredients happened to be in the refrigerator and pantry that day. It was our home, until that night.

We unlocked the graffitied door and entered a house that felt cold and strangely foreign. Those graffitied words expelled us form our own home. Not just from our home, but from the land. This house no longer felt like our home because America was not our home. Although a year before, we swore allegiance under a photo-framed President Reagan blessing us with a grandfatherly smile; although my father gathered us nightly to pray for Reagan because he was God's servant who magically made illegals into legals with a magical pen, signing the Immigration and Control Act of 1986– my father kept the precarious life of deportation-fear to himself for six years; although we had our

5

citizenship framed, and the original pad-locked; although, next to church, there was no other place we went with more regularity and religiosity than Kentucky Fried Chicken, the American shrine where a white Colonel Sanders invited us to dinner for his homemade "finger-licking" chicken; yet America didn't want us to settle.

"Go back home chink."

We were to deport ourselves back to China though we were not Chinese. I immigrated from Korea when I was seven. I had vague memories of it, even more vague emotional attachment. Korea was not my home because I gave up my Korean citizenship when I was sworn in as an American citizen; because it had been 10 years since I've see *Song Tan,* the city where I grew up and I could not locate in a map until years later; because I could not tell you a single Korean poem but I liked reading T.S. Eliot though I could not tell you why back then; because I fought my grandpa, tooth and nail and tongue, who scolded me for losing my Korean because, he said, "language is culture," only realizing as a senior in college that my grandfather lived through the Japanese occupation where they tried to erase the Korean culture by taking away his Korean name and language; because I sang America's National Anthem through its twenty octaves, but did not know the words of Korea's anthem past the first line; because I have never been to China and I did not want to go back to Korea, except for a visit. But America didn't want me to make a home for myself because China is for all yellows.

My father brought out buckets and sponges and we scrubbed vigorously to erase the graffiti; most of the ink dripped off, the outline persisted like a ghost.

* * *

Seeking a home where he himself is free.
(America never was America to me.)

Langston Hughes Let America be America Again

After a year in that house, we moved east across Long Island that extended like a long tilde from the Q of Queens. We eventually went back to Queens where there were more immigrants like us, wandering, Americans in citizenship, but not in color.

* * *

When you are told you are not American enough times, you believe it. We are not reasoned to our beliefs, but shouted into them. The slurs become an inner voice, a consciousness. When your land rejects you, your develop a *double consciousness*. W.E. Dubois coined it in his autoethnographic titled *The Souls of Black Folk* as he tried to explicate the deep rift within him. Double Consciousness, he says, is "this sense of always looking at one's self through the eyes of others, of measuring one's soul by the tape of a world that looks on in amused contempt and pity." Double consciousness is the work of the ghost of the graffiti taking your body, possessing your voice so you are saying to yourself, "Go back home, chink!" Intellectually, you know it's not your voice, but because it's in you, it's hard for you to believe it's not yours. Double consciousness is hating shopping at Macy's on Roosevelt Avenue in Flushing, because your chink-mom will haggle on a dress price, and you hide behind the white, slender mannequins.

Double consciousness is societal-rejection coded into self-rejection. A code that is recoded thousand times a day, in explicit slurs and in implicit projections of normalcy, the white faces of actors, politicians, writers, teachers, church leaders and anyone with power and speaks with authority.

When preaching to a new congregation, I am not introduced as a preacher, but as a *Korean-American* preacher. A true American needs no adjective. A true American is a noun. I am always a qualifying adjective. Double consciousness is the insubstantial adjective.

This double consciousness, this rejection of oneself, is not sustainable. You cannot keep negating yourself, insistently and deeply. You find a way to deal with it. There are options.

You compensate for your double consciousness by doubling your effort to be American, prove that damn inner voice wrong; be more American than any white guy. Change your name from "Kwang Sung" to "Samuel." Push that character-based Korean name into the hidden middle name. Change your last name. Marry a "Smith" or a "Johnson." Work on your pronunciation, roll the "R," so it doesn't sound like that sing-song "L." Lose your need to create an ending vowel as most Korean words; get used to ending in a clean, hard consonant. Become William Carlos Williams, his Carolos's immigrant history safely tucked away with the safe and proper English name of "Williams."

Such bleaching is abrasive, and an erasure. Your Korean name pushed aside, and with it the Korean language, culture, and anything that comes from your parents, and parents too. You lose your heritage, you lose your ancestors.

My grandfather came to America when he got into a motor cycle accident in *Song Tan*, driving 60 in a highway when he was 65. He moved in with us when we moved back to Queens. He often got up from the dining table, tapping his walking cane, and chewed out my brothers and I, accusing us of disrespecting an elder by not speaking Korean during meal time. "You could be cursing me out!?" my grandfather suspected. My parents agreed and sent us to Korean school on Saturday mornings. They wanted us to assimilate, bought us Met's baseball caps, mitts and bats to play pick up baseball game, but Saturday baseball can wait for Korean school. "At least read your Korean name in Korean!" my grandfather railed.

My grandfather was not a sour person. "When he entered a room," my grandmother told me after his funeral, "in a few minutes everyone would be laughing." He was humorous and adventurous. He once bought a pair of hamsters from the street. The pair was a couple and when they had a litter we saw them cannibalize their young. Scarred for life we wanted to throw them out. He kept them. He was also compassionate. But when it came to Korean language, he was deadly serious.

His last words to me were in Korean. He said, "*Nae-il da kkeun-nat-da*" My elementary Korean interpreted it as, "tomorrow is the end." I thought I had a day to make amends.

That day, I shared those words to a friend who had just come from Korea. He offered another interpretation: "My work is done."

My grandfather believed God didn't play dice with human lives. His life was evidence of God the director for he was an adamant atheist until he got struck dumb. He called for the village pastor to sing a hymn, and when he joined the pastor for the third verse, he found his voice again. He breathed because he was tasked. Now, his mission was done. He was putting his house in order; and I thought I had one more day. I never had that extra day. When I begged him for forgiveness, his eyes were locked to the ceiling; he had lost his voice, desperately seeking another breath. I want to believe he heard me.

How could I deny my grandfather? Especially after he left me.

Another option is to leave the country. Deny America. Why stay when you are not wanted? James Baldwin did that for a while, sought a new way to identify himself and went to Paris, where he discovered he was more American than African, that he knew a Tennessee white farmer's songs and soul better than Africans who shared his dark skin.

America gets into you. Though America may reject you, America is alluring, conniving.

It is partly the indelibility of your childhood years. You don't choose your childhood, but your childhood chooses many things for you, what you like to eat, what scares you, who you fall in love with. You do not have to love your childhood – though for you own sanity it is best to accept it — but you cannot hate it. You can't strip yourself of your childhood as much as you can't strip off your body. Your yellow skin is your body and is you, but so is your American childhood, growing up watching Gilligan's Island and Happy Days, and reading Mark Twain and Walt Whitman, and writing to be like them.

I grew up in Flushing, a corner of Queens and one terminus stop of 7 train, and just a stop from Shea stadium years before it was replaced by Citifield. When I drive through it on my way to visit my parents in Westbury, I wonder how I ever survived those streets divvied up by Chinese, Korean and Latino gangs, turning the pain of rootlessness into street fights. I don't want my children to grow up there. Yet, nostalgia surges over me when I read the restaurant signs, *Geum-gang-san, Sam-won-gak*, surviving from my childhood days — Macy didn't. I feel the pleasant nausea of homesickness when I drive by P.S. 20, where I played baseball on concrete and chalk-drawn bases.

You can't leave America because America won't leave you.

I went back to Korea after graduating from seminary. I took a year off before starting church work, to learn Korean, do what my grandfather wanted me to do, my penance. Every time I hailed a taxi and gave the name of the stops, "*Jong-no-sam-gak, Gyeong-bok-gung*" the driver would pin me, "*Gyo-po*," which means an ex-pat, or a Korean gone abroad. It is slightly derogatory. English flaunts itself in every Korean word I say.

Remove double consciousness by silencing one of the two voices.

"You are a chink." Then don't be one. But you can't negate yourself. It's suicide.

"Go home." I will. Leave America, but America is not geography but a way of seeing, doing and speaking, and you can't leave such things behind.

There is another option. Deny double-consciousness itself. Maybe the double-consciousness is not in you, but in America itself. It took a poet to show me this.

* * *

Say, who are you that mumbles in the dark?
And who are you that draws your veil across the stars?

Langston Hughes. Let America be America Again

There is a solace when you find people who suffer the oppression you suffer. So I excelled in the Korean church youth group: president of youth group, then college-advisor of youth group, then youth pastor. They were "my people." I huddled with them often. It's a solace of silence; we don't have to mention our suffering; it's already understood. It's a solace but still a silence.

But your spine straightens when you hear your voice in another's voice. I found my voice through Langston Hugh's voice. His poem. *Let America be America Again*, gave body, nouns and verbs, larynx and teeth, to my voice. I remember reading the poem for the first time and knowing that my life would have been different if I had this poem in my youth. Why wasn't this poem a required reading?

For Hughes spoke out loud what I was whispering to myself, and the inner voices became speech. Inner voices feel like inviolable conscience. You can't reason with your inner voice, only obey. Speech, on the other hand, is presentation of an idea. And an idea, you can explore, understand, disagree with. You can argue and refute speech.

Hughes' poem incarnated my inner voice into a speech.

I am the Negro bearing slavery's scars.

Langston Hughes, Let America be America Again

A poem is not read, but spoken. And speaking is resurrection; the voice of the poet and the voice of the reader resurrect each other. When I read Hughes out loud, I imagine Hughes of my imagination, calm and more baritone than his recordings, reciting his poem without paper, as if he was birthing it for the first time, a creation *ex-nihilo*. After all, he is the "I am" of the poem. But it is my voice I hear, with its deeper timber and tone and the Korean and Queens mutt accent. The words are vibrating on my lips. In my inner ear, I hear the cadence of Hughes, but my physical ear hears my inflections. Hughes is the "I am" of the poem, but so am I. I am also the repeating "I am" of the poem. Hughes channels his voice through me; I channel my voice through Hughes.

And as I speak the poem, I begin to understand because one doesn't understand one's voice until it steps out of the shadow of whisper and into light of sound.

I know. I am not black. Hughes is black.

The *black slavery* experience and the *yellow immigrant* experience are different. The difference is not simple. It is not the difference of individuality, but of history. He has Transatlantic slave trade, arms and legs spread out like a meat in butcher's market for better valuation, and selling away of his children like a bitch's pups. And there is the difference of skin colors and where they fall in the racial hierarchy. Yellow is not as dark as black. Yellow is lighter color and has been held up as the ideal minority, a faux social category created to guilt the black for their ghettos. But we share in the experience of double consciousness, that no matter the length of our stay in this land, we were never seen as true Americans.

Yes, double consciousness has struck the yellows with the brutal club of racist laws too. We have our blues too. Miscegenation laws: yellow cannot marry white because it's unnatural, because yellow is unnatural. Executive Order 9066 where "Japs," though citizens and residents, were herded into concentration camps. Vincent Chin, whose skull was cracked open with a baseball bat and justice put a sticker price on a yellow life: three years of probation. That's the spit-worth of a yellow life. And the rational for releasing the murderers back into the society? They were Americans. Americans were losing jobs to foreigners. Vincent is a foreigner by the color of his skin, so who cannot empathize with Americans fighting for American jobs and American ideals, with guns in Vietnam and baseball bats in Detroit. Patriotism is always in danger of cannibalism, of killing its own citizens and its own ideals. It is America who is the contradiction.

* * *

I am the poor white, fooled and pushed apart,
I am the Negro bearing slavery's scars.
I am the red man driven from the land,
I am the immigrant clutching the hope I seek—

This stanza is in response to inquiry of who are the silent ones, who are rejected and marginalized into silence.

But here is a surprising paradox I understood only as I spoke this poem repeatedly, sounding myself into its meaning. In affirming one's marginalization one's margin becomes a central/important place, a place worth speech, of history, of poetry. In saying "I have been silent," one has already broken the silence.

The "I" is reinstated when it speaks of its dissolution, its enslavement, its oppression, the expulsion of the "I."

I grew up thinking I can get away from the haunt of the slur if I deny that I am the "chink." But the poet Hughes, or as I now call him, prophet Hughes, tells me to own up. I am the chink. When I give witness to my rejection, I find that "I" doesn't die. Silence kills, not the rejection. Speech resurrects. Speech overcomes rejection, the way resurrection is the overcoming of death. Resurrection is not the reversal of death but the break-through of death. And the "I" that goes through rejection is an expansive I. When I affirm my experience, being "poor," "driven," "clutching," "bearing slavery's scars," the "I" becomes encompassing, broad, universal, becomes the poor, driven, clutching and bearing slavery's scars.

When I affirm that I am Korean and that I am American, and that in this body, I am both, then that very confession becomes a declaration, that this body has no contradiction, that double consciousness is not inherent to my body. When I reject the self-rejecting inner voice, then I become the inner voice of America, the conscience that says to America that you haven't been faithful to yourself, that you are you own worst nightmare because you have been faithless to your dream. The tearing of the soul is no longer in me but within America itself.

The poet Frank Bidart writes, "Every serious work of art about America has the same/Theme: America/is a great Idea: the reality leaves something to be desired." Not just art, but history. The history of America is the story of the struggle between the Dream of equality for everyone and the nightmare of its power-mongering, fear-driven racial politics that horded the dream for the elites. "All men are created equal" but not poor men, or red men, or black men, or yellow men, or women. Send me the "wretched refuse of your teeming shore/ Send these, the homeless, tempest-tost to me," but not if they are Irish, French, Germans, Chinese, Japanese, or Muslims.

And not just art and history, but every immigrant or refugee rejected by America is evidence of America's double-mindedness, the shame of America' unfaithfulness to itself. The poor white, the black slave, the yellow immigrant judge America's hypocrisy.

But the judging voice is not condemnation. It is not damnation but a call to repentance. And repentance is the energy of hope, for repentance is a belief that we are not doomed in our sinful ways, but we can choose new possibilities. The immigrant as the inner voice of America does not conspire against America, but inspires America to unfailingly strive to be faithful to its own dreams. Immigrants are the prophets of America. Prophets seek to awake their nation from the stupor of their day dreams – the lies they tell themselves to sustain status quo — so the nation they love can pursue a real dream. Prophets are not doomsayers but dreamers and those who know the American nightmares are the greatest dreamers. So Langston Hughes, a black poet who knows what it means to hate his black skin, walked through that self-hatred and emerged with faith in himself which was big enough to be faith in the very land that indoctrinated him to hate his black skin, a faith strong enough to call American to believe in itself:

O, let America be America again—
The land that never has been yet—
And yet must be—the land where every man is free.
The land that's mine—the poor man's, Indian's, Negro's, ME—
Who made America,

I have that faith because now I know, it is America who needs to come to terms with me; for this is my land; this is my country; and I am home.

Cracks

Beverly Butler Faragasso

I push my husband over the uneven threshold of the room where we will be voting and I am out of breath. I stop in front of a long desk in the room and click the brakes. My husband lowers his feet and stretches his legs.

I show our voter registration cards to the woman at the desk and she shakes her head.

"Don't need. *Name?*""Frank" my husband says and spells our long last name.

"Frank" my husband says and spells our long last name.

"ID?" she asks, holding out her hand and I give her Frank's driver's license.

She checks off his name and points to a man standing in the middle of the room.

"This man will help you with the next part," she tells us.

"Can he fill out the form?" the man looks at me.

"Yes," Frank answers as I push him to a booth the man designates.

Frank's curtain drawn, I begin to walk back to the registration desk when the man stops me.

"Are *you* voting *too?*" he asks.

I *think*, "Hum," but I *say*, "Yes."

During the lag of a few interminable seconds, the man and I do not speak.

"We're *married*," I say into the silence, "We have the same last name."

"Oh."

We look at each other.

"Uh," the man tells me finally, "you should go to the table where you, where you, first took your *husband*."

I hear the emphasis on "husband," knot my lips into a smile, nod and walk towards the front desk.

The ground where I am walking is shifting. Curiously enough, I feel it in both my head and my legs, but it makes my entire body wobbly, unsteady. There is a crack forming in the floor, and I am on one side and my questioner on the other. If this had been the first time such a crack had appeared, perhaps I would not have thought much about it. I probably would not be writing about it now. The truth, however, is that I have had other exchanges such as this one – deceptively subtle, usually, at least on the surface – when a crack also occurs and I know, in part, that it is about race. Frank is Italian/Irish American and I am African American. Couples like us have been able to get legally married for several decades, yet I know that not everyone is comfortable living in the reality of the legislation. But, I also know that this unsteady feeling I have is about more than just the difference in the color of Frank and my skin. A young greeter at a local drugstore, when we lived in Virginia, once asked me, "What's *your* relationship to *him*?" Her question surprised me and I remember taking a deep breath as I braced myself to give her an answer. After I folded Frank's walker to put it in the backseat of our car, a man sitting next to us in the parking lot of a hardware store in Florida, where we live now, leaned out of his window and said to me, "Thank you for the work you do." I slid the walker into our car and thanked him. He continued talking and I realized that he thought I was Frank's *paid* caregiver. After exercise class one day, I went over to where several other exercisers were signing up to bring food for a potluck lunch. When the sheet came to me, I said out loud that "my husband" and I were going to bring fruit. One woman, who usually sits directly facing us during class, expressed surprise. "I thought," she said, "that you were just helping Frank out."

When we were married almost eleven and a half years ago, many of our wedding guests did not know that Frank has Parkinson's Disease. His spine was straight, and he did not need a cane or a walker or even the crook of my arm. On our honeymoon, we held hands as we strolled through town and on the beach, something we often did in those early days and that first year. No one ever questioned – at least not to our faces – whether or not we were a couple. Then, a series of events occurred that changed Frank and me, and, in turn, the perceptions of some of the strangers who encountered us. Three days before our first anniversary, Frank had back surgery. By our eighth anniversary, he had five more surgeries, and, with each cut of the surgeon's knife, Frank's back became more stooped. I am sure that to outsiders, he *looked* like he "needed help." The inquiries into the nature of our relationship soon began. Frank walked slowly and his feet often got tangled as he walked. Parkinson's created a staccato shuffle, making his gait a little stilted, a little uncoordinated. Not surprisingly, Frank also began to fall, often without warning. He started leaning on a cane and went through a number of them before he got his first walker. We held hands less often. The questions continued. While Frank was in rehabilitation following one of his hospitalizations, I ordered a wheelchair. Frank never wanted to be wheeled through airports or anywhere else and he had been adamant about not wanting one in our home, but he agreed this time because we knew a wheelchair might be one way to keep him safe. Our hand holding days were virtually over.

As Frank's body began to fail him and as his needs increased, I did more for him. I went from simply packing his lunch to driving him to work and work-related events. I went from visiting him in the hospital to sleeping on cots or chairs next to his hospital bed. So, all the strangers who identify me as Frank's caregiver are *not* wrong. I *am* his caregiver. What these strangers *get wrong* is that I am *not* paid for what I do, even though I am sure both kinds of caregivers do much of the same work. I arrange doctors' appointments. I am the voice in Frank's ear reminding him how to safely use his walker and I push him when his legs stop working or the distance is too far. I am his fingers when he cannot tie his shoelaces or button his shirts. I drive. I am sure many paid caregivers do these same things. The *difference*, of course, is that I am Frank's *wife*. We live in the same house and we kiss. I send Christmas cards to our family and friends, and I make sure presents arrive in time for Frank's grandchildren's birthdays even though they live half a world away. I host dinner parties. I cry quiet tears when he has had an impossible day. I cannot imagine that these activities or behaviors or feelings would be in a paid caregiver's job description.

This is why I feel a crack, a shift. I am Frank's wife *and* caregiver, but because I am *also* African American, many people cannot put the two together. I think that because they have seen women who look like me taking care of men (*and women*) who look like Frank, they believe that what they have seen before must be what they are seeing now. In the exercise class, for instance, Frank and I often drink from the same water bottle. I sometimes instinctively put my hand on his knee. Frank will sometimes playfully squeeze my shoulders. If I sense that he is losing his balance, I will keep him upright by placing my hand on the small of his back or by gripping the inside of his belt. We even make funny faces at each other, particularly when we are attempting stressful maneuvers! These are the gestures and behaviors of two people who have an intimate relationship, yet a woman who sees us close-up week after week after week has missed these cues. None of the other people in the sign-up group said anything to her like, "How could you think that?" or "Of course, they're married," so it is possible she was not the only person in the group who mis-read us.

When we – Frank and I are included in this — allow past experiences and first impressions to determine what we *think* we see and know about people, then it is hard, almost impossible to change that. I understand this. Frank and I have our own prejudices. Nonetheless, I believe that, we must try to be quiet when we first encounter people who do not or may not fit any "typical" or "traditional" molds that we have seen. It is then incumbent upon us to simply listen and look. I am convinced that, beyond race, beyond physical challenges, beyond religion, beyond appearance, it is in the listening and observing that we truly meet people. Otherwise, I believe we belittle our and their true selves. If a stranger can imagine me as Frank's wife and caregiver, then perhaps she can stretch her imagination to see him as a wrestler and a runner and a historian. Further, if she can imagine us in those roles, she will, in her mind's eye, see us dancing at our reception and boarding a plane for our honeymoon. If the rest of us join her in this imaginative and realistic pull, then we can seal up the racial and cultural cracks that divide us. In that moment, we will stand on the same side of the floor and the ground will stop shifting.

Curious about America

Luisa Kay Reyes

When the hustle and bustle of the school day quieted down and yielded to the stony silence of the dust and small stones settling on the ground after being kicked up by all of the students eagerly heading home for the day, I found myself standing all alone in the middle of the school yard. The sun was shining up in the sky since it was still the early afternoon. And the only other person left in the school's enclave was the security guard who was standing in his office up the steps near the entrance. He stepped out of his office once to check and see if I was still there and then returned to his station, leaving me to explore the school grounds at will. After scouting out everything that called my attention, I found myself once again standing in the middle of the school yard and I took one big giant step forward. I thought to myself, "I've taken one step closer to the USA. Which means I'm one step closer to home." Then I took one big giant step backwards. Thinking to myself that "This brings me one step closer to where I'm at now." I did it again. I took one humongous step forwards and thought to myself "Now I'm one step closer to the U.S., which means I'm one step closer to home." Once again, I followed my step forward with one big humongous step back. With the thought that entered my mind this time being "But this is where I'm at now. This is my home." It was quite a curiosity for me.

I was a little girl attending the very prestigious Southern Annex of the Colegio Aleman Alexander Von Humboldt in Mexico City. The German School as we often called it for short, was a very highly sought after academic institution with the bulk of the student body being comprised of the children of German businessmen, a few students who were half-German and half-Mexican, and then some Mexican students who came from affluent families eager to have their children benefit from the school's excellent education. Since there was also an American school in Mexico City, most of the American expatriate families attended the American school. While it was considered a good school, the students who failed out of the German School would transfer to the American school, where they would skip a grade and still be at the top of their class. Often times without having ever had a day of English. With my mother being a teacher and coming from an academically oriented family, she opted to forego the American School and we were one of two American families who attended the German School. As such, we definitely stood out and I found myself quite curious about the whole American thing.

In reality, my father was Mexican. But he wasn't around and while I took after him with my very dark hair and eyes, I had inherited my mother's fair skin. Which would lead to the people in our neighborhood often referring to me as "blanca" or white. But at our School, some of the German parents would comment to my mother on how dark-haired I was. For at the German School, some of the students were so blonde that their hair appeared to be nearly white even though they were little kids. At times, some of the German boys wore their whitish blonde hair spiked up with gel and one could even see their red scalp underneath. All of this prompted me to ask my mother one day why I wasn't blonde. Since in those days my mother was a platinum blonde with sparkling big blue eyes. And while my brother's hair would get as dark as mine when he got older, at that time he was the charming little blonde boy. I don't remember what my mother said, but I do remember that in my mind my mother symbolized America to me. Everywhere we went, she was "la gringa" or the American lady. And since I was curious about America, I just felt the mighty USA was synonymous with my mother. The problem was, that it didn't always seem to be so.

We would attend the American Churches on Sundays. First we attended the American Baptist Church and then we switched to the more staid Union Evangelical Church in Mexico City. One day, a middle-aged or so American couple at the Church was promoting an American celebration that this organization they were a part of was having. They put up fliers in the Church and talked about it every chance that they could. Since they really espoused the event so very heavily, my mother decided to take us to it. When we got there, they were serving Americanized Mexican food, even though we were in the land of plenty as far as real Mexican food was concerned. The chef for the event was tarrying quite a while in preparing the dessert which was arroz con leche, the famous Mexican rice pudding dessert. And everybody was standing around waiting. I happened to walk past the kitchen when the door was open and I saw the chef taste the dessert as he was cooking it and then dip his spoon right back into the big pot and continue stirring the rice with his taster spoon. I told my mother about it and she wasn't too pleased. But we decided to wait on the dessert, anyway.

Most of the people in attendance appeared to be older American couples. But one fellow, decided to try and be friendly and initiate a conversation with us.

He came up and asked my mother "Which branch of the armed forces did your husband serve in?" It turned out the event was put on by expatriate U.S. military families living in Mexico City. And my mother had to explain to him that her husband hadn't served in any branch of the military. We were there because the couple at Church had practically begged everybody to come. The fellow then made his way to talk to some other people after that and I suddenly had the feeling that in spite of us being at an American themed gathering, we didn't really belong.

Most of the time at school, I was referred to as the American girl. Although, this wasn't always in a positive context. One day as we were working some crossword puzzles in class, I decided to fill in the little squares in the print handwriting I had seen when we were in the States. Since we would go to the States nearly every Christmas and summer vacation to visit my grandmother in Alabama and then my grandfather in Ohio, I would pick up on some Americanisms every now and then. At the German school we weren't taught how to print. Right away from the beginning we were taught to write in cursive using our blue ink fountain pens. My brother and I loved our fountain pens! We would collect the little white balls that were left in the ink cartridges after they were out of ink and in every class there was always somebody who had more of the little white balls than everybody else. In my class, the leader in collecting the little white balls was a boy and it seemed like to the rest of us that he must have kept every white ball we had ever used from kindergarten on up. He was quite proud of that fact.

At the end of our class, after we had turned in our papers and our teacher was grading them. She called me up to the front and told me "You did the crossword puzzle using the American handwriting. That's interesting." Even though she didn't tell me not to, I felt that she wasn't too pleased by my choice of writing. And I never wrote in print again.

A few times at school, I was the Mexican girl. Since the school day was taught half in German and the other half in Spanish, we had faculty from both nationalities. It was an unvoiced common thought among the student body that the German kids were the smartest ones in our school. Looking back, I can see that they had the advantage with the language. But none of us stopped to think about that at the time. Instead, we would eat raisins during our recesses because the rumor was that raisins would make us smarter. One of our favorite games to play in class was the "kopfrechnen" in which the teacher would line us up in front and then quickly ask us something along the lines of "What is four plus eight, half-that, plus seven, and double-that?" We would have to spout out the answer quickly in these mental math games without using any calculators or anything of the sort. Some of the kids would try and use their fingers behind their backs to figure it out, but that was the slowest way to come up with the answer. If they were able to do so at all. The quickest way was to simply envision it in one's head. Whomever could come up with the correct answer the quickest and most often, would then be declared the "Königin" or 'König' of the kopfrechnen. This was something in which I really excelled. I really enjoyed the kopfrechnen and I would always be the "Königin" or Queen of these mental math games. The fact that I would beat even the full-blooded German students in these games was a source of pride to my Mexican teachers who for the moment at least, would consider me Mexican.

Sometimes at Church, I was considered Mexican, too. One Wednesday evening at the American Baptist Church, we were there for the Church supper. They always had really good tostadas there, but this time things were running late and the kitchen was closed. There were still some left over tostadas in the buffet, but for some reason they weren't letting anybody have any of them. As young kids always are, my brother and I were hungry and my mother sent me up to get one. There was a girl in front of me who was American and the serving lady wouldn't let her have any. She happened to be Mexican and when it was my turn, I asked her if I could have one. She nodded in agreement and said that since I was Mexican, I could.

Back in school one day, our teacher was leading us in a discussion on why the Spanish conquest of Mexico hadn't yet produced a world superpower like the British conquest of the USA. It was a weighty discussion to be sure. And our teacher told us that when the Spaniards came to Mexico, the Indians had so much gold that they just plundered the gold from the Indians. On the contrary, when the British arrived in America, there was no gold to be picked up off the streets. To make a profit, instead they had to plant tobacco and other crops which involved them investing in the land and growing an affection for the land. The lesson for us, according to her, was to invest in Mexico and love our country. As always, when America's status as a prominent world power was discussed, there was a tremendous amount of tension in our class. After our teacher finished her initial lecture, one of the half-German and half-Mexican boys in our class spoke up. He heavily favored his very handsome father and he had visited the States recently. With much distaste in his voice, he announced that he had seen a lot of trash piled up in valleys along the side of the road. I had seen that too when we visited the States, as it was just before the Adopt-A-Mile and other environmentally friendly projects came into vogue. Since he was the class heartthrob every time he spoke, his words carried a certain weight to them. And I couldn't deny that aspect of his statements. However when he said he didn't think the USA was all that great. After all, they had trash problems, too and the whole class agreed with him, I pondered his logic for a moment and simply remained quiet.

One day when we had come back from visiting the States, I wore a wristwatch that we had gotten in the USA to school. It was lavender and had a square cover over the actual watch part that could be folded out into the shape of a doll. My classmates all clamored to see this latest American toy of mine and they begged me to see it so much, that I actually grew a little bit weary of having to fold it out and show it to everyone. During our class break, a couple of girls begged me to see my watch and to avoid having everybody beseech me for the same, I hid behind the side of the building and showed it just to those two girls. Immediately when we sat back down in our class after our break was over, another girl hollered to me that she had heard all about my watch. It folded out to reveal an Auburn-haired doll with a smiley face and two arms and two legs. It was true, that was how it was. But, I found myself struck by how quickly she had already found that out. The rest of the day, the big news item at school was my new American watch.

It seemed like whatever item was considered to be the latest American fad was always in style among our classmates at our school. One time it was the Garbage Pail Kids trading cards. A spin off of the popular adorable and fluffy Cabbage Patch dolls, these cards featured some grotesque versions pulling big gobs of snot out of their noses and other such things. They were absolutely hideous. Yet, incredibly popular. They were quite the fashion and our school was completely flooded with these cards. During every recess everybody would proudly show off which cards they had and make deals to obtain the cards they didn't have. My little brother and I weren't impressed by these cards and actually didn't have any. But that still didn't deter my classmates from showing me theirs, even though I didn't care to see a single one. Our school didn't approve. And within a few days, they sent us all home with a letter stating that if anybody were caught on or near the school grounds with these cards during or after school hours, they would be expelled immediately. When I showed my mother the letter, I thought she would be happy. After all, I had heard her express her disapproval of the ugly things to some of the other adults. Instead, when she finished reading the letter what I heard her say was "They wouldn't be able to do that in the States." I wondered why. But, I never saw another one of those cards again.

I frequently overheard the adults talking about how corrupt the government was and how the politicians would steal all the money. So as I stood in line waiting for my coin to be handed to me, the thought occurred to me that if the politicians stole money, it couldn't be while she was on duty. For the government lady who was handing out the coins to all of us kids was very serious, very strict, and very professional. While all of us kids were all very excited, we felt we had to contain our glee somewhat since she came across as a very exacting person. Truth to be told, she was probably just doing her job well. For we had turned in a 100 pesos coin the week before and now the government lady was here to hand each of us a 1000 pesos coin in return. The rumor was that it was all part of a project on the part of the government to teach us kids to believe in and invest in the government. There was much commotion about this project, but the main thing on our minds as we stood in line was what we could buy with it at the school store. Most of us kids were wanting to buy some of the delicious molletes, a white toasted bun with refried beans and some white cheese on top. It was a simple Mexican dish to make, but the molletes at the school store were the best ones in the whole city. At least, that's what all of us standing in line that day thought.

When my turn came to stand in front of the government lady, she double-checked to make sure my name was on the list and then handed me my brand new coin. Right away I noticed how shiny it was and how the copper hue gleamed even though the lighting in the room was dim. Of course, I quickly joined the other kids who were rushing to the school store, but by the time I got there, it was closed. Naturally, I was disappointed. But when I walked back to where everybody was standing, I noticed the adults were all clustered around my mother. With all the parents listening to her, including even several of the Dads, my mother vociferously stated that she "just didn't see how the government could afford to do that." This handing out of the coins seemed like a preposterous notion to my mother. And as I took my place beside my mother, I was curious about the fact that everybody seemed to be paying special attention to what my mother was saying. I don't remember what became of my coin. However, I do still recall how shiny it was.

All of a sudden I felt myself trembling in my seat at my desk. Our favorite teacher, Frau Brechtel, had walked in with a very serious look on her face. Immediately stilling the light-hearted right before class conversation of my classmates. We didn't know what to think. We had had Frau Brechtel as our teacher a couple of grades before, so we knew her well. But, whatever this was, it seemed like the world must be coming to an end. In all earnestness and with all of us staring at her in all solemnity and wide-eyed, Frau Brechtel proceeded to take her place in the center at the front of the class and with her head held high, told us that we were now old enough to know the difference between "tener clase" and being "corriente." That is to say, knowing the difference between "having class" and being "cheap and common". We were positively frightened. She explained to us that she wanted us to be sure and correct each other whenever one of us used a word that was corriente and always be on guard ourselves to make sure we always had class. It was something we definitely took to heart. And one time, I even corrected my best friend Fabiola when she used the word gente, which means people. It wasn't a bad word or anything along those lines. I just simply felt that the classier sounding word was personas or persons. She accepted my correction and we continued playing like always.

Then we went to Church and there was an American man standing in the front holding the microphone with his two sons. His two sons were wearing shorts and standing slump-shouldered. They appeared to be completely bored by the fact that there were up there and the word on everybody's minds was that they were definitely American. Once again, I was curious. It dawned on me that the American School must not have a Frau Brechtel. And I wondered why they didn't.

With my brother's birthday being three days before mine, I nearly always knew what my birthday presents were going to be. We were close in age and my presents were often a pinker and frillier version of whatever my younger brother had gotten for his birthday. As we were riding on the train from the border to Mexico City, I told these hearty college aged all-American boys what I thought my presents were going to be. I guessed one of my presents was going to be one of the popular tent-like coverings for my bed similar to one that my brother had gotten. And one of the American fellows told me that they would be there to help me put it together. I wondered why he would say that, but I dismissed it. My brother and I were quite little. But since we spoke English, the American boys seemed to gravitate towards us on the journey. Even to the point of putting up with my birthday present chatter. When we finally reached Mexico City, my mother took on the role of the local hostess and helped them decide where to go and which sights to see and so forth. One of the boys had drunk so much on the train, that when we got off at the train station, he heaved and heaved so much, it was miracle he didn't throw up his entire stomach and intestines in the process. My brother and I couldn't believe it was possible for someone to throw up so much. Once he finished heaving everything that he could, the American boys got into their taxi and we headed to our home. To our surprise, shortly after we got home, the American boys showed up. They claimed the taxi driver had taken them for being a bunch of ignorant gringos and was really overcharging them. So they decided to just come to our house.

My mother graciously invited them in and they proceeded to put together our tent beds, since I had guessed correctly. For my birthday I received a pink princess castle tent bed while my brother's was a blue race car shaped tent bed covering. The American boys were all quite tipsy and even though they were adults, my brother and I noticed that they seemed to struggle to put together the plastic pieces. But, in all fairness, after what seemed to be a long period of time; they finally were able to put them together and they were all quite happy. After they were done, the one fellow turned to me in all seriousness and said "See, I told you we would be here to help you put it together." He was a man of his word, he told me. And I got the impression that meant a lot to him. In fact, I was so struck by how important it was to him to actually do what he said, that instead of saying "Thank you", I remained silent. The American boys left shortly after that.

Every week there would be a street market that would set up in our neighborhood. It was a good place to shop for fresh fruits and vegetables at reasonable prices, but some of the vendors also sold other knickknacks such as shoes and other household items. One vendor this time around had a lot of towels. My mother could drive a good bargain at the market most of the time, but this time my mother suddenly started exclaiming over this one towel. It was red, white, and blue and featured big letters that said "USA." My mother was just so excited and I didn't know why. She was even bouncing out of excitement as she turned to me and very spiritedly said "Look, Luisa, USA!" Only, she was speaking in Spanish since we were at the market and the "U-S-A" sounded like "oohssah". I told her that I didn't know what that was. "Of course you do!" my mother responded. But, somehow I wasn't catching on. I merely shrugged my shoulders and looked on as my mother just went ecstatic over this towel. Rarely had I seen my mother so excited about something and I was curious about why a simple towel would be eliciting such an effusive response from my mother. Then, when I was less than a month shy of turning ten, we moved back to the United States of America…and my curiosity was satisfied.

"Okie Dokie"

Kristen Mai Pham

A few months into our relationship, Paul casually commented that I often used the term "okie dokie." I replied, "I like to say okie dokie because it reminds me of Mom".

When I was young, I was embarrassed by my mother. She was so different from the other moms and she spoke very broken English. She had no idea what a cupcake was, so when it came time for school bake sales, she always came up empty-handed. To make things worse, I was forced to wear unfashionable yellow and red striped sweaters that she seemed to love knitting. I thought that she was so uncool. Sadly, I was too young to understand that my mother was actually a hero.

My mother was the only surviving child of my industrious, widowed grandmother. Mom grew up in comfort, which continued when she met my father, a wealthy self-made man. Dad lavished her with expensive jewelry and gifts. After marrying Dad, Mom's afternoons were filled with hosting luncheons for bourgeois guests, having her nails done, or hiring new nannies and servants. She never needed to lift a finger because she was a delicate socialite. The most upsetting experience of her life had been a "sports injury" that she acquired. Apparently, she had hurt her wrist while playing ping pong. This story still makes me chuckle to this day.

Mom's life of privilege was abruptly ripped from underneath her when the communists overthrew the existing government of South Vietnam on April 30, 1975. Our beloved home was no longer our home. Mom, Dad, Grandma, my siblings, and I had to flee the country. We barely made it out, with just the clothes that we wore and fear in our hearts. We had lost everything.

Beset by chaos and unrest, we boarded a dilapidated boat to escape from our war-torn birthplace. The ride on this boat was emotionally exhausting and physically dangerous. I remember asking my mother if we could go home because the drinking water on the boat smelled like gasoline. My mother simply replied, "We can never go home again so please drink the water, Mai". She must have been devastated, terrified, and grief-stricken but she did her best to remain calm.

I am told that some people may have perished from starvation, sickness, or exhaustion on that boat during our long journey. But not my mother. This delicate socialite held onto her will to survive in that dark, damp, stinking boat.

After what seemed like an eternity of sea and air travel, we eventually landed in Camp Pendleton, California. Through a Red Cross/Catholic Church sponsored refugee program, we found a home in Orange County, California where Mom's life changed drastically again.

Mom had to learn to speak English in record time. America was a big, scary country where everything seemed to move at lightning speed. Learning to drive a car on the California roads became a seemingly insurmountable task for Mom. But she learned to navigate the streets and she drove wherever she needed to go: the Asian grocery stores, Pic'n Save, and to her first job.

Given the reality of our newfound poverty, she took a back-breaking job where she did assembly work for hours a day. If overtime work was available, she always welcomed the extra money. On those days, she arose around 4 AM and worked very long hours.

Work life was not easy for her when she was subjected to racial prejudice. Being a Vietnamese refugee in 1975 was no easy task given the unpopularity of the war. Some people would call her names and make fun of her English. She often broke down in tears in the break room. Although this was an awful time for my mother, she forged on.

After a full day's work, she cooked authentic Vietnamese meals for us from scratch. Then she would clean the kitchen so that she could start all over again the next day. This exhausting cycle continued for years.

Miraculously, Mom managed to feed our family of six on a weekly grocery budget of only $ 25. And somehow, she still found a way to save money. Mom knitted sweaters to keep me warm in the winter and sewed light dresses to keep me cool in the summer. She truly learned the value of a dollar.

Despite the hardships of her new life, Mom still managed to maintain a sense of humor. She would make me laugh with her funny exaggerations: "It's so hot my head is going to explode" or "I'm so hungry that my stomach disappeared".

Despite the cultural differences, Mom learned to enjoy the simple pleasures of American life. She loved TV so we often watched her favorite shows together. She could not pronounce Jack Tripper so she referred to the lead on Three's Company as "Zack Tripper". She giggled at the sight of Boy George during his TV appearances as he sang "Do You Really Want To Hurt Me?" When I asked if she wanted to watch I Love Lucy she would reply "okie dokie" with a twinkle in her eye.

My mother stood by my father's side and together they rebuilt our lives. They purchased a home on a very limited budget. Her children attended college and went on to lead productive lives. Not bad for a former delicate socialite who really couldn't speak English, drive, or cook.

Words cannot express the gratitude that I have for my mother. I thank her for being exactly the person that she was. I thank her for the hardships that she endured. I thank her for instilling me with high standards and the will to persevere. I thank her for being a wonderful, strong mother who loved me dearly no matter what I did or said, no matter how unkind or unthoughtful.

My mother survived a fall from the highest mountain and managed to rise up from the abyss, rebuilding a foundation that was stronger than ever. When life got crazy, my mother rose to the occasion beyond everyone's wildest expectations. And she did all of this with a loving spirit. If that isn't a hero, I don't know what is.

Given the hardships that she experienced, my mother could have easily become hardened. Anyone else might have given up. But she didn't. Her "okie dokie" seemed to embody her will to survive. It was her lighthearted response to a sometimes menacing world. For her, it meant holding onto your optimism when life throws you a huge curve ball.

Mom passed away six years ago. In the grand scheme of things, whether she spoke broken English or couldn't bake a cupcake is totally irrelevant to me. What is relevant is the lasting impact that she made on my life.

To me, her "okie dokie" is synonymous with courage, strength, sacrifice, love, laughter, and ultimately, triumph. It is one of my favorite phrases because it encompasses the core being of my amazing mother.

(Motor)Home

Dheepa Maturi

"Ma'am, are you sure you want to take those with you?"

My aunt nodded vigorously, clutching four bath towels with one arm and the leathery Cherokee with the other as he supported her plump form. He watched the remaining ten of us clamber to the water's edge with varying degrees of grace, given that two of our party wore silk sarees, three carried towels, one lugged camera equipment, and yet another held his cigarettes and lighter at the ready. Most of us couldn't swim a lick.

We were going white water rafting.

Three minutes after launch, our towels were sodden, and the cameras and cigarettes, jettisoned. My panic-stricken aunt insisted on maneuvering to a narrow side ridge and then scrambled out, whereupon the hapless raft, now freed of substantial weight, shot down the river corridor. Simultaneously, she and her husband stretched their arms out to one another, Bollywood movie style, shrieking each other's names while the flummoxed Cherokee shouted, "Just stay there, Ma'am! Just stay right there!"

Many years I later, I watched National Lampoon's *Vacation*. When they made that movie, they chose the wrong family.

* * *

The entire trip was the brainchild of Chandra Uncle, ever the hatcher of bold plans.

Chandra Uncle's family and mine felt a powerful bond from having immigrated contemporaneously, and also as distant relatives for whom geographic distance from the motherland had obliterated true familial distance. Of course, it's possible my parents had never considered the relationship distant — after all, Chandra Uncle's wife was the sister of my father's brother's wife. Without fully comprehending the exact relationship, I'd nevertheless absorbed the fact that we were all *close,* and his children were my "cousins" as far as I needed to be concerned.

31

That particular year, our two families were hosting mutual relatives from India — what an opportunity, Chandra Uncle said, for all of us to *experience America!*

He rented the largest motorhome he could find — I won't say "RV" because it was nothing like the tricked-out luxury behemoths of today — which had a capacity of eight. (There were eleven of us.) We handed our cash to the owner, and, with nary a contract to be signed or a lesson on motorhome mechanics to be imparted, we stepped aboard our vacation-on-wheels, pungent with co-mingled odors of rug shampoo and stale smoke, ready to hurtle down the highway, separated from the outside world only by four walls of (we were soon to learn) questionable structural integrity.

As unprepared as we were for day-to-day motorhoming, we did have a plan: drive south from Ohio to Tennessee's Ruby Falls and the World's Fair; camp, play, and take in various and sundry sights along the way; and then terminate our trip in Gatlinburg before the return journey.

I don't know how the eight adults adapted themselves to the cramped quarters, but we three kids, ages 10-12, discovered and appropriated a small nook with a table, ostensibly to play SlapJack, but actually, to lay plans to steal and destroy our uncle's disgusting cigarettes and also to subject everyone to that singular torture, "99 Bottles of Beer on the Wall."

Within twenty minutes, before we could administer the aforementioned torments, eleven heads rose in unison when sounds began to emerge from the engine compartment — *bang, bang*…sputter-bang-bang. That was the first time.

It was not the last time.

* * *

Nasty public showers (ten), injuries (four) and vehicle breakdowns (five) aside, this trip is a shining memory of my childhood. Every aspect was an adventure — from sleeping sardine-like in narrow bunks to buying miniscule boxes of detergent to eating breakfast cereal out of paper cups. At the World's Fair, I proudly ascended the New Technology stage when a boxy robot asked for volunteers, though I think I accidentally broke its skinny metal arm when it asked for a high-five. At one of the fair's country booths, a kimono-clad lady painted my name on a tiny piece of rice, which I promptly lost — probably because I suspected she didn't really know the translation of "Dheepa" into Japanese.

It was indeed an experience of America, an up-close-and-personal foray through a part of this vast and variegated country we had not yet seen. Against a traditional backdrop of mellow Southern accents, Appalachian terrain, and seriously starchy food (we struggled valiantly for vegetarian cuisine and subsisted mostly on variations of potatoes which we sprinkled surreptitiously with chili powder brought from home), we also witnessed America's overlap of cultures — evidenced not only by our own immigrant presence, but also by the tourists at the World's Fair and Ruby Falls and Gatlinburg, all following multilingual tour guides, taking in the sites, and shopping for kitsch.

Looking back, it is also a memory of myself at my most innocent and idealistic. During that motorhome journey, I lived my actual understanding of America: the place to which a person brought her heritage and placed it in the open-armed embrace of an open-minded country, a country that joyously welcomed all. I experienced a natural extension of all of those beliefs, and I drank in the cedars, poplars and amber waves of grain, felt welcomed by everyone we encountered, and never once registered a bemused, confused, or hostile glance, though I'm sure we earned more than one.

At that time, even with my brown skin and Indian heritage, I felt 100 percent American. In school, I'd read about and identified with the brave Pilgrims and the courageous Columbus. During the winter concert, I'd proudly belted out cloying verses of nationalistic songs proclaiming that every one of us, regardless of race, religion, or country of origin, belonged in the United States of America.

Admittedly, one incident did mar my otherwise enchanting trip. Chandra Uncle was incapable of passing a sign proclaiming "World's Largest Waterslide" without stopping the motorhome. The other adults, much wiser after our first water endeavor, firmly passed on the opportunity, but we kids grasped the proffered foam mats and mounted several hundred stairs. What I didn't know was that the World's Largest Waterslide was comprised entirely of concrete, so both of my forearms, reflexively trying to slow my breakneck progress, clamped down and ultimately lost most of their skin. I landed a bloody mess and carried the burns for the rest of the trip, but, more than the pain, I remember my shock — my searing disappointment in what had seemed so welcoming.

During the years following the trip, realities began to counterbalance my understanding in pace with my maturity. Columbus may have been courageous, but I also learned the effects of his behavior and actions on the natives he encountered. I learned that the descendants of English escapees of religious oppression later burned women at the stake, fearful of their communion with the natural world. I slowly grasped the consequences of a country's enslaving an entire race, of its extirpating its indigenous peoples.

The same textbooks that fed me this information had a darker side. They referred to my country of origin as ignorant and backward and claimed it would be a miracle if it could ever feed itself. They ignored centuries of colonial rape that had decimated the wealth of one of the richest nations of the ancient world and disregarded its thousands of years of culture, civilization, and philosophy, as well as its colossal contributions to world consciousness by way of yoga and meditation.

My classmates, influenced by equally inaccurate portrayals in the media of the time, asked whether I ate eyeball soup or sacrificed humans or worshipped rats. Some asked me to identify my tribe, though that sort of ignorance hurt less. I'd like to say I quickly and consistently refuted all the erroneous statements and bizarre questions, but eventually, their sheer accumulation made me turn away, shame bubbling. Over time, I became too tired and embarrassed to battle.

It was my most difficult lesson growing up: even if I embraced the people around me as my American brothers and sisters, not all of them would see me in the same light. Rather, they might see only the brown and braided one, whose family members wore dots on their heads, who hailed from a pitiful, primitive place. I began to comprehend racial slurs and to realize they were directed at me. I cringed as kids pretended to pull out the pins of hand grenades, throw them at me, and then shield themselves from the purported explosions. My parents revealed they'd been refused service in restaurants, that they'd received anonymous letters threatening our family and admonishing us to return to wherever the hell we came from.

In college, I studied the instability of recorded history and the ways victors, colonizers, and oppressors harnessed language to tell their stories and characterize their victims. In fact, the precarious connection between history and truth became the subject of my senior thesis, the culmination of the sadness of the ten years following my motorhome journey.

Throughout those years I wondered why many cousins and friends in larger cities, even those just five or six years younger than me, did not seem to face or feel the same torments. Perhaps there were larger numbers of minorities in their towns and schools. Perhaps, within a few short years, popular culture gradually absorbed and displayed sufficient bits of Indian culture to ward off potential assailants — Bollywood dance contests, henna tattoos, brown faces in movies and TV shows, "Jai Ho" piping through shopping center music systems.

* * *

I think of my child self, the girl who had the chance to feel and experience her ideals first-hand while roving America in a motorhome. She visits my consciousness from time to time, especially as the country becomes more complicated, its politics more dysfunctional, its race relations simultaneously more nuanced and more incendiary, and as conversations proliferate about who belongs here and who needs to be forcibly removed.

She is the one who reminds me of my awe of the social experiment that is America, an experiment stunning in its scope and its appeal to human nature at its most inclusive and accepting. She recalls my admiration of the forefathers' decision to set standards so altitudinous that achieving them could only be a journey — a Herculean, and perhaps even impossible, one.

And she reminds me of my sheer gratitude for having grown up here, for having received such opportunities and experiences, for having met people so openhearted, so desirous to learn and understand, and so cognizant of the hybrid vigor and blended beauty of this visionary place. I am thankful, too, for the perspective my life here provides vis-a-vis my own cultural heritage, for the space it grants me to examine and choose the principles and standards that fit my life and my family, and for this fertile, fecund, in-between space I occupy.

My love is no longer innocent, like a child's. Rather, I love this country like a spouse whose failings I must forgive, over and over, whose many kindnesses and virtues I must remember and cherish over our long haul together. And I love it like a parent who honors good intentions and efforts, who believes in potential and promise, and who excuses missteps and disappointments — every time.

days like this

Shanita Bigelow

The beginnings of madness are subtle, listless even, harmless (we think): slight change in dress, attitude, behavior, slight change in the way we see what is to be seen, hear what is to be heard. Everything changes (vision blurred, voices stammer into being, collide like ill-fated memories into visible light, stilled darkness, that retreat) and, despite the changes, we say nothing. I remained silent, watcher of webs spun in my name and image. It bothered me but not enough to talk about it, until it was too late. The beginnings (yes, there are many) trickle in unnoticed, a small crack in the ceiling of our lives.

Ceiling, symbol: the color said to prevent nesting. It did not. Corners pressed: twig, leaf, other debris—awnings filled with spring sound.

Each year provides various starts and ends: New Year's Eve and New Year's Day, the start of spring and the end of winter, your birthday and the day before, other religious holidays, astronomical shifts, moon phases, sunrise and sunset, your alarm clock. There are other lists, your own included, and they are often longer than we assume. These markers of time gone by are those cracks, weathered, rusting metal, water damage, wrinkling skin. This is life, we imagine, but it is always more shift than constant, more crumpling than wrinkling, and we are alive. Through it all, we live with a sense of normalcy, sometimes dignity, most of the time grief and anticipation: Who am I? What has been lost to memory? What's next?

What life began in those corners, it finished inside.

It is 2016. What is real? Is there no plot against darker bodies? What is uncertain today has always been uncertain to many: tomorrow, the promise, the threat. And I feel the need to run, splinter again into a mess of probable, of normal (what is expected of us, that sense of dis-ease James Baldwin described as a kind of schizophrenia). I won't name it. I can't fully describe it, but I will always bear it. What we witness in ourselves, that internal reflective surface, free of regret, guilt, the haze of probable outcomes we see blurred, distancing itself from all we perceive to be us as objects before a camera or in a rearview mirror, becomes a signal, a beacon to those around us, a call to all that we are and have always been (here).

Inside they could not rest. Always awake and sounding, doubt crept up like a familiar. It needs to be said. Notice them. Potted plants, an iron bench, 'welcome' inscribed on their faces: the porch became site of new rites, rituals to be performed in early evening hours.

My mother stood there in the dark, so many years ago. I must have been three or four. Scooped into my father's arms, out of waking, he carried me to the screen door, implored her to come back inside. She said nothing, stood still, hand on railing, profile hardly perceptible in the haze of one street light. Only now, as I write this, am I aware of the thickness of that silence, it's impenetrability, his pleas, my confusion, that door. A screen and a panel of glass, wire mesh, that barrier between worlds (it seems). Always inviting, outside seemed a haven, a means of escape even if fleeting. But that wasn't always the case.

One afternoon (it must have been summer), we were playing in the backyard. I was old enough to fight back, to fight for myself, but I didn't. A boy from next door came to play with us, me. He picked up the plastic jump rope and began to hit me with it. I stood there stinging in the driveway while my father looked on from inside, on the back porch, through the screen door. I cried and asked the boy to stop and eventually it ended, but I don't remember how. All I remember is wondering why. Why had I done nothing to stop him? Why did my father stand there watching and do nothing to protect me? Why had I refused to fight?

There's no escape, no true way out of hell unless you face every layer of your fears. We wish for a guide. We want Virgil to take our hand and lead us through the fire and ice, but he's gone. He treads his own journey, and we must find our own way.

I am not afraid to see them through. Call forth paint chip and cobweb gods, little creatures we'd known as passable. Passing through, wind finished their work, left pleading each breath, light in whispers. They are not dead yet, only beginning to flower. Let them in. Let them out. Speak.

Days like this are repressive. It is 2016 and sunny. Days like this are perfect for destruction, implosions of all kinds and death. Days like this should come with a warning label: 'Caution: gentle breeze may lull you into, may camouflage the panic beating in your chest.' Days like this I wonder where the clouds have gone, the heavy ones, where the wind and rain have disappeared to. And then I realize it has been ingested, and the storms brew within us.

I am a woman born of this land who will not claim it. I am a dark soul rushing to be released. I pour. I drown in the onslaught. There will always be days like this, days that allow for the perfect storm. Days where fear paralyzes tongue. I am a black woman in America. It is 2016. I am in possession of myself, a self not long ago (un)willfully (dis)possessed. Days like this prepare me for the storms to come. On days like this, I am reminded of another some years ago. It was 2008. It was a beautiful day, but I was a wayward wind, a single dark cloud in a sea of white. I was an isolated shower of fear, panic, paranoia. That day, I was the eye of the storm.

Outside everything shimmered, impenetrable veneer of ease. Inside I felt none, though I was aware of the breeze, the sky, trees. Inside, what was viewed as another day on the campus (students milling about, chatting, smiling, upright) was translated by panic into a feeling of overwhelming distrust for those faces, all white, for that sky, so blue. I was acutely aware of my race. I have always been aware, but this was different, this moment put me on guard, made me pay close attention to others' movements, facial expressions, mannerisms. I was fearful, suspicious.

Aphids borrowing, from the last of them, a kind of hunger unmatched, passable. We are mistaken. Awnings swept, corners emptied, silence. We do away with possibility as soon as they begin to speak. Utter a name, fragrance, watch them settle soil, attempt to take root. Broken eggs, cracking blue, ceiling became portent. Ceiling took the blame, hardened.

If the ceiling was a person, could ever be, it would be my father; the walls, my mother, and the floors, every layer, my brother and me. We were the home we grew up in, and as the walls began to shift, the ceiling always at a precarious tilt, the floors, while they sometimes creaked, were never unsettled.

Home: the first of many places where I had to face my fears. There were the spirits (sentient shadows), bugs (crickets, spiders, horseflies, lady bugs, etc.), sounds (wind, leaf-crunch, speeding cars, silence) and always a sense of uncertainty. The ceiling would often appear to cave in, subjecting the whole house to its fragility and doubt.

My father was violent, often angry. He was also very funny, charming even. I loved him dearly. There were times when it seemed as if he'd crumble but wouldn't show it and instead, would subject us to his clinging to, grasping for posture: I don't remember my exact age, but I was in second or third grade and we, my father, brother and me, were watching *The Making of the Lion King* on ABC. There was a lion loosely drawn and glittered on my blue and purple tie-dyed t-shirt. There was little lion in me. My father asked me a simple question: 'Is daddy fat or skinny?' He wasn't fat. 'Skinny,' I proudly proclaimed. Wrong. The consequence of this game was not a deduction of points or losing out all together; it was further questioning, louder and louder as if the answer were my face or my very being. I went outside where my mother raked leaves. I sat at the picnic table. I probably cried, though I don't want to remember it that way. There were no words. Nothing to be said other than, 'Your dad?' I nodded.

Why? Why did I believe I was wrong, that he was right? Why did I question the validity of my answer but not the validity of his anger? Why was there this latching to control, this calculated assault? Is this very individual, this very specific instance dissimilar to the capitalist fantasy we are purported to live in? Was my father, am I somehow not a symptom of its power, greed, façade? This is what we consume, this need for normalcy, to not only have it, but create it and control it. My father did bad things, but I never viewed him as an inherently bad person. However, never knowing how your right will be accepted, if at all, is not a great feeling. My mother, often outside in these memories, sustained most of the wounds, wounds I was not entirely witness to.

Catastrophe: When I felt the yanking of my strings and their multiplication. When there is a sound not far off, but too distant for distinction. When I told myself she was wrong. When the customer is always right, especially if she is your mother.

One school break, home from campus maybe my sophomore or junior year, my mother and I went fabric shopping. The upholstery on the dining room chairs, which had been there for as long as I could remember (longer than that) needed to be replaced. We were in line to check out or get the fabric cut and the woman behind the register or cutting table said something, it could've been anything, but it was disrespectful and aimed at my mother. Again, paralysis kicked in and I muttered something, but really, I did nothing, I said nothing and was embarrassed not for my lack of words, but for my inability to, once again, protect my mother. We left the store relatively unscathed and reupholstered the chairs. Well I did. Some of the chairs have the fabric on right side up, the rest have it on wrong side up. We couldn't decide which was better, both striking and beguiling in their own way.

It seems life is this way too: what is upside down, turned inward, inside out, all that we attempt to hide, to settle into, finds its way to the surface, and sometimes it's (as my mother would say) halfway presentable. That is, it can be withstood. It's managed, dealt with and through our becoming/coming to terms with it, it transforms, is perceived as presentable, maybe even lovely. What does that mean? There's a saying that the sharpest, the strongest sword is forged through fire, it's impurities hammered, seared away. As a child, I often felt as though all my rough edges were being slowly sanded smooth through the coarse, the roughness of my father's voice, his implosions, his regrets.

I don't remember him ever saying sorry. There were no words, no need for an apology. I knew he did not like what he did, had done. One Sunday morning, we got in his blue Ford pick-up. I wore frilled socks and black patent leather shoes, a dress. My brother was probably there too, but I don't remember that. I remember walking into church, sitting on the wooden bench, eyeing the bible in the back of the bench in front of me. My mother was not there. She stayed home that morning. Perhaps there was an argument. Maybe she was tired. I don't know, but when service started and the preacher (a woman) began to speak of love and family and forgiveness, I looked at my dad. He wore these big rusty brown red frames. He removed them to wipe away his tears. He nodded as she continued to speak, and he cried. I've seen men nod loudly, silently agreeing with some lesson aired, spoken of, as if to convince themselves. Those nods of awareness, of (perhaps finally) acceptance of wrong doing that can't be undone, alert me to the fact that we all wish we could take some things back.

Catastrophe: Not being responsible. Opening the door to strangers that are really strange and probably have bad intentions. Closing doors. When there is no other way to say no. Apathy. Not speaking up.

I'm not blaming my family for my break, for that day in 2008. My mother is caring, very kind and funny. Uncertainty: that's where I'm going with this. I would question myself, my reality even as a kid, and while I was happy—I had a very happy childhood (close friends, girl scouts, sleep overs, scavenger hunts, learning to bake bread and cookies, camping, after school arts programs, sports, etc.)—there were times when I questioned everything and could answer nothing.

After the divorce (I was in elementary school), things were tough on her, but it never felt that way for us (my brother and me). We had everything we needed and sometimes things we wanted. She worked full-time during the day, 8:30AM to 5:00PM. At 6:00PM she reported to her part-time job. She'd return home around 11:00PM or 12:00AM. We'd have food prepared and bath water running for her, but sometimes we'd be asleep or at least try to.

And I'm lost again. I don't know exactly where to go from here—that is, I have nothing to complain about, no need to bely guilt or regret. I sometimes believe that we are living the lives we've chosen to live, that what has happened needed to in some way. But sometimes I believe life is not fair and what has happened didn't have to.

Catastrophe: Denial. Betrayal of self/reason. Monster vision. Lack of sleep. Sharp teeth sharpening. Giving up. Erasing the drafts/refusing to. Forgetting. Avoiding. Being unprepared. Faking it. Missing a button. Not willing to iron your shirts. Not willing to do anything more.

It's 2008. Fall is steadily becoming winter. It's darker than expected at certain hours. I am living alone in a studio apartment a few miles away from campus. I'd never lived alone before. When the symptoms began, they were not symptoms but feelings I've always had. Times when light is harrowing and people terrifying, times when self-doubt redoubles its efforts, and I'm paralyzed, overwhelmed with the possibility of life in any other fashion. I didn't realize I was eating less (I'd lost 14 pounds), that I spent more time sleeping, more time in the dark; I didn't realize I was sad or anxious, that I spent more time alone. I thought, believed I was lazy, that it would pass as it always did, that it was normal. I'm afraid of normal.

Catastrophe: Settling. Reducing your emotions/pain/confusion to hormonal changes or a chemical imbalance or someone else's; those things or other things that have nothing to do with your feelings/emotions/confusion. Refusing to listen to the silence between. Refusing to read what has been written for your benefit.

Normalcy is a fallacy. What we experience routinely becomes normal. What we see emblazoned on screens, working its way out of others' mouths is our prediction, our estimation of normal. But it's just another construct, another tool for division, for relinquishing what personal power we have to the auspices of becoming that, anything other than what we are, what we experience, our normal.

Catastrophe: Taking what is not yours from someone else who took that something from someone else. Elephants are not for. Thinking you deserve something/thinking you don't. Thinking that that thinking is wrong or that it shouldn't be (exist/wrong). Assuming anything.

Once all that time in the dark became irregular thoughts, thoughts of being followed, of my family and friends in danger, of racist plots against me and people of color, once it became an unwillingness to move, I was still able to see. It was something to be dealt with, something to deal with personally—that is, on my own. It was that sense of normalcy that I was afraid to change (in part). I know. It doesn't make sense. As my mind, the functions, the disorder has come to light, so too has this failing sense of normalcy. What is possible? I have seen this dis-ease (but never called it such) as my only means of existence for so long. I was afraid of what was possible. No one should be afraid of possibility. Don't be afraid of possible.

Catastrophe: Desiring weapons like elephants and shears or nylon and menthol or pity or grammatical errors and tongues or acrylic and sawdust or toothpicks and pickled things or Bubble Yum and extension cords or packing tape and plums or grits and animation or The Sandlot. Assuming any of those are weapons.

I ruined *The Sandlot*. For a good stretch, it was one of my favorite movies, watched and rewound, watched and rewound and watched again. We sat down in the living room to watch it as a family. Someone put it in the VCR (probably me but maybe my brother) and we readied ourselves. Wrong. All that watching and rewinding had stripped the tape, had distorted the first few minutes. Waves of color. Static. Black and white. It was all fuzzy, and it was my fault. You don't damage good things, I learned at a young age. Things cost money and money is never certain, so you take care of those things as if their place, their return is never assured.

Anything can be a weapon, I also learned. Anything can be used against you, can be made to prove you wrong. Maybe that's the thing that I sometimes think is not fair.

When it started in 2008, I was uncertain of my being, of what I was doing with my life, where I was going, what I would do. I had no answers and was terrified of the nothing encircling everything. I wasn't sure of my own memory. My brother sent me a birthday card. It was supposed to be funny. In hindsight, it was pretty clever: made upside down, you opened it, were disoriented. The text was also funny, but I don't remember what it said. I do remember the monkey on the front and what my brother wrote (also very clever and kind), but I was not in the right state to receive such cleverness. Everything was literal or inherently symbolic in my paranoid frame. So, I believed the joke and thought my entire life was a lie, that I'd somehow just come to to realize nothing and everything was in shambles. It was hilarious, part of the big joke, the one designed to make me scramble and squirm. Funny shit.

Disguised in normalcy, ask of what it means to fight. Ask them whose left. Ask them what they've done to your brothers, to their children. Ask them to break open your back, slice it down the middle, dissect spine, lungs, kidney, pancreas.

It's 2016. I know how old I am. I know where I am. I am lucid enough to see the devastation, natural and otherwise, that we deem normal. The truth is, I'm not a conspiracy theorist. The truth is, those threats, though seemingly absurd at the time, are not entirely. For some, they are very present, very real. They come from all angles, all relations, all spaces. Some are blatant reminders, other less so.

My father was a threat. I'm sure at some point in his life or many, he felt threatened by someone or something. As I attempt to understand him, fully, I am forced to reconcile the whole of him with the hole left in his absence. What pressures, internal, external, grind down on a man, already weathered, to the point of extinction? I'm a threat to some, and I honor that. Because what threatens is sometimes fuel for the threat, at other times to be feared. The truth is, those things I feared for myself and my family are realities in the United States, all over the world. Don't dismiss my panic, my anger, my pain, my fears. They do not have to be justified, but they are.

Whittle your way through bone. Nerve endings, nerves like strings, but energized, electric can recall too.

And I feel like that is what has been handed down to me, not blood or memory but bone, the hard stuff you can't fully absorb or relinquish, and I am grateful for it. Our history, American history, has been whittled, carved out of a stone found in the middle of a large river, perhaps the Mississippi. Whatever its name, the rock of it can never be itself again, not fully. And I'm abstracting the thing that must be the heart of this, whatever it is. History is not real, but imagined facts turned apostle. It is a reality, a construct of the past that we chew and swallow as if our only means of sustenance. In the history of this country I call home, many, many lives have been lost (needlessly) for the sake of what we call democracy. I don't believe in it. My father was not a democracy, nor was he truly part of one. I'm not a democracy, though I wish to understand fully what that can mean. The bone: the strength of a human is not measured in the weight they can handle, but in the way that weight is measured in their mind.

Men are the bone and flesh of new times. Women are the blood and bone, sinew and tissue of all time. How do we measure the facts of our existence against the facts of our collective memory? The threat: it's not what humans can do, physically, to other humans, to all life, but rather, the capacity of humans to subject the mind to a construction of the facts so narrow and prescribed it becomes them. What does that mean? We know the stereotypes. We believe in some of them, but rarely do we measure their aim and consequence. Ida B. Wells outlined, very specifically, in *The Red Record* (1892) what this means. Her work is not done, because the threat(s) that did my father in (a lifetime of ill-advised anger, perhaps regret, drink and sorrow, his health, his love, his words and attempted song, racism, discrimination, a lack of understanding, an unwillingness to) have a history of their own. Just as individual as he was and just as broad as we (humanity) are.

Nerve endings, nerves like strings, but energized, electric can recall too. Ask me to define conspiracy. Ask me to describe reality. Ask anything of anyone. Please. I cannot feel my fingers.

Before, during and after my break (though not now, thankfully), my fingers and toes, when introduced to temperature changes and/or stress, would adversely react, in that they would do the opposite of what they are designed to do: keep me warm. It's called Raynaud's disease. It's amazing how the body reacts to both the external and internal worlds, and I wonder what that means for all life, particularly human life. What is it that we have absorbed into our beings that cause paranoia, panic, undue stress, anger/rage, sorrow? We have many names for this dis-ease, but we name everything. And I wonder if the damage is done in naming.

The limitations of our language to describe the interconnectedness of body and mind, of person to person to institution to construct belie a certain indifference, a certain distance from reality. My delusions then, in 2008, have returned and gone and returned and gone, and I feel they will never truly dissolve, especially given the present circumstances. The denial of difference as a means of communion creates in us the desire to separate, to discover in difference a distaste for what we perceive ourselves not to be.

Ask anything of anyone. Please. I cannot feel my fingers.

"Here" and "now" are contested grounds. The future, too, seems perilous. Given the present state of the country, the dire need for a pause in vitriolic rhetoric, disingenuous facades, and superficial appeals to all Americans, we are forced to, very concretely, focus on the "here" and "now." Any investment and investigation in the present requires an acute and sobering look at the past. How have we gotten to this point? And, more importantly, where do we go from here?

What does this moment, in my very ordinary life, have to do with the incredibly violent and unnecessary deaths of young men and women of color? Why write about that moment eight years ago, now? For me this was just a moment. Imagine if it were a day, a year, a lifetime. That fear, that indescribable feeling I felt then, on that perfect day, shook me to my core. I am still attempting to recover. But this is not about me. What I am failing to articulate, what I am working toward understanding is not the contradictions of that day, but the inability to describe that feeling. Call it paranoia, panic, confusion. Call it heavy, demeaning. Call it cowardly. Call it shame or courage or perspective. Call it whatever you'd like and know that now, at this very moment, I feel it again. And I want to be able to describe it. I want to understand why death has and continues to come to so many of us, people of color, young people, young men (in particular). Why are our lives, our bodies, such a point of contention?

It's easy to point fingers, to place blame. It's simple to say that we must better train our police officers. We must address both conscious and unconscious biases. We must move past surface tensions, America, and address the undercurrent. The shooting deaths of so many are not merely the acts of troubled individuals, or ill-equipped police departments; it is the continuation, the amplification of a system as old as this country, older. The question then becomes, "What can I do about it?" What are we to do? I don't have the answers, but I'd like to posit this: it's time to truly dissect and analyze our troubled/troubling narratives.

I'll start by giving you part of mine in hopes that I may one day hear, see, read part of yours and then maybe we could talk. Maybe we could discuss their common seams, threads or whatever image/metaphor you want to use to describe your story, your history as it's woven into the fabric of our collective memory and history. This is not a simple answer. It only serves as a platform for even more complex questions, many that we may not be able to answer in our lifetimes, so I write this with the hope of it outlasting my own biases, my former and present self, the pain and confliction that comes with every life, every family, our shared history.

Strange sensations, your body, a brain on fuzzy things and fond memories. This is your brain on brains, your brain riddled and disintegrating, your back, a board game. Do you know them? Why do they need me here? Why am I unsure of what was first, what was mine, my own mal intent? Do you? If so, ask them to free her. Mona Lisa. Mona lisa, mona lisa, mona lisa. Turn on them and tell me how it feels.

On days like this, I'm reminded of days gone by, of my childhood and younger adulthood. I'm reminded of my life thus far, and how on days like this, the silence is unbearable, the loss of hope seems imminent, but then I pick up the phone or I write these words and they give me pause—"Who am I?" I ask. "What on earth am I doing?" As I attempt to resolve these questions of living, I think about the fact that that is all we ever really do: always on the spectrum of understanding, of figuring it out. Now I ask myself, "What are we doing to ourselves?" My response, my resolution is inaudible; there are no words to describe what we all are inevitably feeling, as if the wind were knocked out of us, as if suddenly waking from a dream.

I'm tired of weathering the storm of my consciousness, tired of careening ever deeper into the chaos of these times. I'm tired of telling myself I need to rest, to sleep, to heal as if this day was a wound. It is, simply put, another day. What are you up to?

Backyards

Rebecca Redshaw

It's amazing the things you find when packing boxes to move. Luckily, this time the move wasn't mine, but my sister's. I'd moved a little over a year ago, and continue to look for lost gems and stumble across junk I can't believe I saved. Ah, but she found a treasure.

Yellowed and frayed around the edges and without a cover lost long ago, an old piano book entitled, "Personality Songs," appeared at the bottom of the stack of papers. "Classics" no one has heard in years, and in all probability, not that many people heard when published. The song titles popped off the pages and triggered memories. Tunes that you can readily imagine upon hearing the titles; "Don't You Want a Little Doggie?" "I Don't Want to Play in Your Yard," "I'd Love to Be a Monkey in the Zoo," "Mamma, I Gave Away the Baby."

When I was a child, my mother played and sang these tunes and more from this book as I snuggled next to her on the wooden piano bench. The last thing I needed was more stuff at my house, but I couldn't resist. I took the book home.

Now, sitting alone on the same piano bench, probably somewhat older than my mother was then, I turn page after page noodling the keys down memory lane. Selective memory is a wonderful thing and I'm sure it helps most of us get through life but I was astounded rereading the lyrics of "Stay in Your Own Back Yard." I remembered it as a sad song, but even in the 50's, when I was just a kid myself, the thought of a child being shunned by other children in the neighborhood just because his skin was a different color didn't sit right with me.

The song is only two verses long with a chorus of the boy's "mammy" telling him "stay on dis side of de high boahd fence, an honey, doan cry so hard." In the second verse the child dies and the woman sings the song to his memory. Tough stuff for what in its day was probably a pop tune. It took me a little time to decipher the Roman numerals of the original publishing date as 1898, which helped explain the use of the word "pickaninny." Other than that obviously unacceptable label, the content of the song could have been today.

I marvel at how people verbalize that we have "come so far" in accepting the differences of one another. The color of one's skin is an obvious separation. Even someone with minimal intelligence can normally divide the black checkers from the red ones on the board.

You don't have to be a genius to look into a room of strangers and note some appear different than others. Some are men some are women, usually easy to tell, but not always. It used to be that shoes would answer the question of ambiguous sexually, but a lot of women are getting savvy to the concept of comfortable shoes equating to comfortable feet. Facial hair is another reliable tipoff, again not foolproof, but worth a wager.

There are other visual dividers that we as humans feel commanded to point out. It's a high probability when a morbidly obese person walks into a room that he may be either ridiculed or pitied for being other than the norm. Or for that matter, staring when someone really tall (not everyone plays basketball) or really short (not everyone wants to join the circus, either) walks by. Gay or straight is a real crap shoot with stereotypes not being reliable at all if one spends anytime in the mountains of Colorado with wonderful heterosexual, outdoor women or with New York hairdressers that pattern themselves after Warren Beatty, in the 70's film, *Shampoo*.

Sometimes differences are ostracized by cruel people who for whatever reason think that because they are momentarily in the majority that makes them superior. More often differences are noted and then seemingly ignored with indifference or tacit politeness.

This fall I went to a Big Ten football game, the first game I had been to in maybe fifteen years. I love football. I even understand the game so I looked forward to watching two good teams perform in a stadium filled with more than 90,000 loyal, supportive fans. About halfway through the first quarter, I looked at the expansive crowd all bundled in school colors clapping rhythmically to the cadence of the band. Looking over the sea of faces, I realized nary a black or brown face was to be found in the crowd. Of course, looking down to the field of play, more than two-thirds of the sixty players on each team were young black men sweating, running, and tackling much to the enjoyment and thrill of the crowd.

I couldn't help but wonder if these players didn't live a similar life to the young boy in the 1898 song. Are they allowed to play within the confines of this "backyard", but nowhere else? Would these fans welcome a player over for dinner when out of uniform? Walking from the bus stop to the front door, what are the chances a nervous neighbor calls the police to report someone who doesn't belong in the neighborhood? Are we still stuck on either side of "da high boahd fence" fearing something we can't explain?

Maybe little by little we inch forward. I'm not sure. I remember my niece at age eight visiting me in California, swimming in the neighbor's pool with their maid's charcoal skinned daughter. In the backyard, I heard Kathy exclaim, "You're so lucky, you don't sunburn." Oh, if we could only acknowledge the differences with the honesty of a child, not be fearful of them.

There are differences. Why not acknowledge them? Learn to know a person – what a concept. Learn that the 300-pound man who waddles into the room writes poetry or makes furniture. Maybe the six-foot-tall woman is a computer genius or maybe the gay man can bench press 350 pounds.

The last tune in the index of Personality Songs is "Won't You Come Over to My House?" This lyric is a young mother singing about a blue-eyed child and about all the toys left in her home since her baby died. Roman numerals, again. 1906.

Ironic, isn't it? Mothers lost babies and children to disease during the turn of the century. We are more than a decade into another century and mothers are still losing children; not so much to fever and plague as to hatred and hopelessness, sometimes in the shape of a bullet, sometimes in the shape of a pill. Black, white, brown, red, yellow; that surface difference doesn't really matter when a child dies. But we'll never get to know one another if we "stay in our own backyard." The world's too small. We'll have no place to go.

Fiction

An Outsider

D. A. Hosek

I don't know how the story about the witch began. It came from nowhere one day; by the time school let out, it was all any of the kids talked about. I was not part of the in crowd, or any crowd really, so I learned about the witch only by overhearing my classmates as they whispered to one another. Everyone, it seemed, was going to the house where it was said she lived to see if they could spot the witch. I wasn't immune to the lure of the unknown; I was going too.

It was November, that empty time between Halloween and Thanksgiving. Everything was dead or dying: the grass, the unraked leaves covering the lawns, the naked trees. The decorations that made Halloween seem festive had transformed into something more menacing, the squirrel-eaten remnants of jack-o-lanterns gave off an odor of decay while paper skeletons, torn by wind and soaked by rain, left ghostly images imprinted on the sidewalks where they had fallen.

As strong as the pull of the witch might have been, I was even more drawn to the scene by the presence of Julie Miller. I had been in love with Julie since we kissed on a dare in kindergarten. To me, that kiss meant that we were bound together forever. For her, that kiss was something that she forgot about by the end of the day. As we grew older and the first tentative

pairings formed between the boys and girls in seventh grade, she chose Frank O'Brien, the bad boy of the class, the kid whose dad rode a motorcycle and drove a semi. How could I possibly compete with that? As much as I wanted to, I knew that I could never measure up.

It seemed like the whole school was at the house three blocks from the school. In reality, it couldn't have been more than twenty or so kids including some of the little ones who had no reason not to believe in the witch. I half-believed it myself even though I should have been too old for that. I wanted to believe. I wanted there to be magic, to be danger, for there to be amazing things in the world. I wanted a world like the one I found in the books that I read at the side of the playground while the girls admired the boys who weren't me in their feats of grade-school athleticism. In a world like that, I might have a chance to be somebody.

There was a surreal mix of the festive and the sinister about the scene. The reds, blues and yellows of children's coats contrasted with the browns and greys of the landscape. It was easy to imagine a witch living in the house before us. There was a chain link fence right at the sidewalk with a mailbox on a pole just inside the gate. Everything in the yard was dead: the grass, the trees, the bushes. What had once been flowers decomposed in raised beds on either side of the front door. Even if we hadn't heard that a witch lived there, we might have imagined it from appearances alone.

I stood just apart from the main group, my glasses hidden in my shirt pocket, in the vain hope that sacrificing my vision would make me somehow cool. It was with this blurred perspective that I sought in vain for what made a girl from the third or fourth grade scream, "There was a green face! And a shotgun! I saw it!"

With those words the younger children on the scene fled home to pretend that they had been brave. Even some of the older kids disappeared, although most of them had left earlier out of boredom. I put my glasses on to try to see the face but saw nothing. The glasses returned to my pocket. I was part of the small group left. Besides myself, it was Frank, Julie and some of Frank's friends.

I think it was Rob Vitek who threw the first stone at the house. They had decided to try to make the witch come out, although the house was far enough from the street that nobody's volleys made it more than halfway across the lawn. I didn't throw any rocks myself, but I did nothing to stop it. Instead I kept staring at the house secretly hoping that there was a witch inside. Maybe she would come out and curse Frank and his pals, and Julie would rush to my arms for comfort.

Nothing like that happened. While the house was obstinate in its inactivity, Frank's friends dared each other to open the gate and walk up to the front door. No one had the temerity to take the dare. Maybe we all believed the girl had been right and there was someone in the house with a shotgun.

I didn't challenge anyone to enter the yard. I ignored the taunts that I was too scared to go myself. Instead, I said something.

"The house is against the alley."

Six words. Stating an obvious fact. But it had somehow escaped their awareness. And it was enough to move us to the back of the house.

The alleys were still unpaved back then: limestone gravel over a bed of mud. A strip of weeds that the town periodically cut to keep them from being a nuisance separated the puddle-filled ruts made by the cars.

Only a two-foot apron of concrete separated the house from the mud and gravel. The yellow paint of the house was flecking off, exposing a dirty white layer painted closer to the wood siding. A storm door had once protected the door to the alley but it had blown off long before. The exposed wood rotted where the hinges had once been.

"I wonder if you can see anything through the curtains," Jimmy Chesnik said. He approached one of the windows.

"Can you see anything?" Rob asked.

"Your mom."

"Funny." Rob frowned, but the other boys laughed. Even I smiled.

"You can't see anything," Jimmy said stepping away from the house. "The curtains are closed and it's dark inside."

I took off my backpack and rested it against the garage on the other side of the alley. What was I doing there? I didn't belong with them and my presence wasn't keeping Frank's arm from Julie's waist, his fingers hooked on the loops of her jeans, even if I tried to convince myself that she wasn't comfortable with how his pinkie caressed her just below her belt.

"You should try the door," Rob said.

"Why don't you?"

They dared each other to try the door. I saw it as my chance to show that I was not just smarter than all of them but braver too. "I'll do it."

Everyone looked at me. They had forgotten that I was there. Julie pushed Frank's hand from her waist, took a step towards me then stopped. I had done it. I'd shown myself a better man than Frank. Now I had to take the next step. And the step after that. Walk to the door. I kept hoping that something would stop me. Maybe one of the cool kids would say something about how they shouldn't bother and we should all leave. But nobody said anything. Not even Julie, although she looked at me with what I hoped was concern.

I reached out for the doorknob. I told myself that it wouldn't kill me to turn it. It was probably locked anyway. I twisted the knob and the door swung open.

I stepped inside and a gust of wind blew the door shut behind me. My knees felt weak.

"Who's that?" a woman's voice called out from another room. She sounded young and different somehow. Her voice was smoother, more elegant than the Chicago-inflected accents that I grew up with in our suburb.

I looked around the kitchen. The interior stood as a sharp contrast to the exterior. Everything was clean and organized. It could have been anybody's kitchen. Next to the sink, a saucepan, bowl and spoon dried in the dish rack. On the table, a basket of fruit stood in the center of the white and gold Formica top. The kitchen was dark because of the drawn curtains, but otherwise was ordinary.

"Is there somebody there? Who's in my house?" The woman's voice grew louder and angrier.

I should have left then. I realize now that I was guilty of breaking and entering. At least of entering. Would that be trespassing? I didn't leave. I walked to the living room where the woman had risen from her chair.

"What do you want?"

She was a young black woman in jeans and a sweater. Her hair was wrapped in an orange silk scarf like a turban. On the table next to her chair was a book, open and face down. The cover was all blurry shapes and unreadable letters courtesy of my uncorrected vision. There was no shotgun.

She looked at me, her face a mixture of anger and curiosity. "Well?" she asked.

It was the first time I'd ever really talked with a black person. I'd seen black people on TV, or when my parents took me downtown to the Loop on shopping trips, but that didn't really count. I'd never been in one of their homes. I somehow expected it to be different. In the early '80s, Mudd Lake was all Czech and Polish and Italian and Irish. Integration was something on the TV news. How could I have known that black people lived in houses just like my own with dishes and refrigerators and fruit and books and tables and chairs? I stared dumbly at her then said the first thing that came to my mind.

"Are you the witch?"

"The witch?"

"The witch."

She looked at me, her mouth open. She couldn't believe how stupid this white boy who had walked into her house could be. "What makes you think that I'm a witch?" she asked.

"You live here, right?"

"Yes."

"Everyone says this is a witch's house."

"Well everybody is wrong. I live here with my husband. Neither of us are witches. Do you believe me?"

I put my glasses on and stared at her. She was beautiful. I hadn't thought of black women as beautiful before then. I tried to remember if any of the black women I saw on television or in the city might have been as beautiful as she was.

"My husband grew up in Mudd Lake."

Her expression changed. She realized what I didn't understand until I was older and had replayed the story in my head many times. It wasn't merely the appearance of the house that had targeted it as a witch's house. The fact that there was a black woman living in Mudd Lake was enough to anger some of the town's residents. And if her husband grew up in Mudd Lake, then he was white, which made things worse. Was it deliberate that some adult had told children that there was a witch in this house?

"What are you staring at?" the woman demanded. "Get the hell out of my house!"

I ran from the house frightened and uncomprehending. The door slammed behind me and I leaned against the garage across the alley to catch my breath. I stared down at my backpack while the others spoke. I couldn't meet their eyes.

"He's back!"

"He's not dead!"

"What happened?"

"Are you OK?"

"Is she all green and ugly?"

"What about the shotgun?"

"What's it like in there?"

"Does she have a big black cauldron?"

I looked up at Frank and Rob and Jimmy and Brian and Julie. Most of all at Julie. Was that admiration in their eyes? I had done something none of the others had been brave enough to do.

And then I ran out of the house like a frightened child. Scared of a young black woman who was angry that I walked into her home like I owned the place. She had every right to be angry. I couldn't tell them the truth about what happened. I didn't want to go back to being the worthless outsider. I didn't realize that any admiration they felt for me would be short-lived.

"What did you see?" Julie asked.

"There was a witch. And she was ugly. But it wasn't a shotgun, it was a broomstick."

Why hadn't they seen through my lie? They were all old enough to know that it couldn't be true, to know that witches weren't real. We all were old enough, weren't we?

If they knew, it didn't stop them. They paid no attention as I ran down the alley and they shouted insults at the house and pelted the windows with rocks from the alley. I turned the corner out of sight from them and bent over to cry as the sound of breaking glass came from the alley.

Letter to my Grandmother

Chang Shih Yen

Querida Abuelita:

¿Cómo estás? How are you? It has been a long time. I miss you. It is getting cold here in San Francisco. The few trees around are changing colour, and the leaves are slowly falling to the ground; but it's not only the weather that is cold. I think the people are cold too. I miss your hugs and your kisses. They always make me feel warm inside.

We all have our Green Cards now, so that's good news and a huge relief. We don't have to worry about getting deported. Though with that *idiota* in charge, it seems anything is a possibility. I know no one wants to be deported, but I think the only good thing about deportation is that I would get to see you again.

I looked on the map, and the distance between us is 1179 miles in a straight line. *Tan lejos.* That's so far, so many miles. But it's not just the distance. On the map there is a thick, black line that denotes the border between USA and México. The thick, black line that divides us. And I know along that black line there is a wall between us too – an actual, physical wall that divides us. Now with that *pendejo* President in power, the wall is probably getting longer and higher. It makes me feel even further away from you.

School is going OK. My grades are quite good actually, but I haven't been here long enough to make any friends. Because I have no friends, I don't go out. And since I don't go out, all I do is stay at home and study. That's why my grades are good. Even if I did have friends, Papá probably wouldn't let me go out with them. You know how strict he is.

You see, the problem is I'm too Mexican to hang out with the popular girls. They are the tall, thin girls with the straightened long, blonde hair. They look like they just walked off the beach. Around them, I'm too Mexican: short and dark, with my brown skin and dark brown eyes, and very curly black hair. You know my English is good, but to these girls I still speak with an accent.

At the same time, I can't hang out with the *chicanas* who have just arrived from México and barely speak any English, because apparently I'm not Mexican enough. Whatever. Just because I'm not crazy about *banda* music and what's happening on the latest telenovela, suddenly I'm not Mexican. To these girls, I'm the *gringa* who's not interested in wearing butt-lifting jeans, as if that's any criteria for how Mexican you are. I worry that in future I will be too Mexican for the US, while at the same time, too *gringa* for México. I will never fit in anywhere. Then, what will I do? I wish you were here Abuelita, so I could talk to you. I'm sure you would give me some advice on how to make friends. I don't need many friends; just one good friend would be enough. It's lonely not having friends.

As you know, I had my 15th birthday party recently. I wish you could have been here for it. Well… maybe not, actually. It was possibly the smallest, most depressing *fiesta de 15 años* ever. I don't think I even have 5 friends that I can call on to be my *chambelanes*. So Mamá found my *chambelan* for me, someone I didn't even know. His name's Ramón, and he's the son of Mamá's work colleague's cousin, or something like that. Dancing with him was painful, in every sense of the word. His hands were all sweaty and gross, and he kept stepping on my feet, which really hurt!

For the changing of the shoes part at my birthday party, I got these pink high-heeled shoes. I slipped off the ballerina flat shoes that I was wearing and changed into the high-heeled shoes, and suddenly just like that, I'm a woman now! The high-heeled shoes were a slingback, peep-toe style with a pink bow on top. The peep-toe style made it even more painful when Ramón with his big feet, stepped on my toes, because there was no protection for my toes at all. My poor toes. The shoes have a 3-inch stiletto heel. The first time I put them on and stood up, my ankles wobbled. I can hardly walk in them, never mind dance. I know these are supposed to be my first high-heeled shoes, but do they really have to be so high? The dance with Ramón didn't go so well, what with shoes I can't walk in and squashed, stepped-on toes.

Then, there was the dress that matched the pink shoes. Mamá got me my *quinceañera* dress. Mamá just does not understand me. How could she possibly think that I would like a pink dress? I'm not sure that bright pink goes with my skin tone and black hair. It was a long, pink dress with sequins and tiny sparkly beads hand sewn on. To me, it says 'drag queen' more than *quinceañera*. It had a sweetheart neckline, gathered in at the waist and then a big, full skirt with ruffles and layers of lace and organza. Under all those layers was a skirt of stiff tulle to give the dress its big shape. I looked like a giant meringue wearing it. I have enclosed a family photo taken at my birthday party. There's Papá, Mamá, *hermanito* Leo and me. I'm the one who looks like a slightly deranged Mexican Barbie. Luckily, you only turn 15 once in your life and I'm glad that it's all over.

Papá says this is a better life than in México. But is it, really? Maybe it's better than working in the fields, or in some kind of sweatshop *maquila*. But I see Papá and Mamá working minimum wage jobs cleaning and waitressing, and I know it's a struggle. The rent here is so high, it's crazy. I'm thinking of getting an after-school job to help out. It's hard to make ends meet, even with both Papá and Mamá working. Papá says we need to do this to have a better future, but I don't want a future without you in it.

Do you know what I miss the most? I miss the long, lazy Sunday lunches at your house, where the whole family gets together: Tío Manuel, Tía Rosa and all the cousins. I miss the food, when your dining table is groaning under the weight of all that food. I love it when I don't know what's for Sunday lunch. It's like a surprise. Maybe it's carnitas – juicy, tender pork with chillies, so spicy they make my tongue tingle. Maybe it's frijolitos, or maybe it's birria. Your birria is my favourite. Mmm… you make the best spicy goat. It's like there is a dance going on inside my mouth.

I like how you let me eat chicharrones in all their crispy, crunchy, porky goodness. You don't mind if I want to eat them for breakfast, lunch and dinner. I love them in a tortilla to make tacos de chicharron, or I can even eat them by themselves dipped in spicy chilli sauce. Yum! If I try and eat chicharrones here, Mamá will be all like, 'Think of your health. You want to get a heart attack and die? You want to get fat?' Of course I don't want a heart attack, but I don't care if I'm fat. I would rather be a *gordita*, fat and happy eating what I want, than be a *flacucha*, stick-thin but hungry and miserable. Anyway, I know you'll love me even if I'm fat.

It will be Day of the Dead soon. This year, we will be baking *pan de muertos* separately again. It's another year where we won't be building altars together, and I won't be able to go to the cemetery with everyone and wait for all our family to come home. I won't be able to scatter a bright path of marigold petals in the cemetery, a bright orange and yellow guide to lead all our ancestors home.

Do you know what I remember, Abuelita? I remember sitting on your lap as a child, over your ample skirts. My first memory is of us in the kitchen, and I'm helping you make tortillas. You let me make little balls with the *masa*, which you press into tortillas and then cook on the *comal*. When I got a bit older, you let me make salsa by pounding all the ingredients in a *molcajete*. It was lots of fun. When I was sick, you brought me your homecooked *caldo de pollo* to help me get better.

I like it when it was just the two of us; we sat next to each other on the sofa listening to the music of Vicente Fernandez on your radio. You stroked my hair with fingers that still faintly smelled of lemon and chillies from your cooking. My hair was a big mess; it still is now. I hardly ever comb it. Curly hair is so hard to manage, but you stroked my hair, running your fingers through my hair and gently untangling my curls with your fingers. And while you stroked my hair, the voice of Vicente Fernandez accompanied us: *Y volver, volver, volver a tus brazos otra vez… quiero volver.* And return, return, return to your arms again… I want to return.

Sometimes we sat on the swing outside your house, just sitting staring at the mezquite trees in the distance, or the maguey plants in the backyard. It was so peaceful, sitting together until darkness fell and then we were looking at the first stars in the night sky. It's funny, but reassuring, to think that even though we are far apart now, we are looking at the same stars in the sky. I will come home one day…*algún día.* Please wait for me. Until then, *te extraño mucho y te quiero mucho.*

Tu nieta,

Lucía

Poetry

assumption of accent

Carl Palmer

I know you'll like this one,
grinning into his racist joke
after hearing my southern drawl.

At the Zoo, February 2017

Heather Lee Schroeder

Maybe this is how   civil war starts—
that recognition that you'd   sooner
put a bullet   through someone's heart:
than let them stare at   your brown son
like that.

You who puts bees and wayward wasps
outside if they wander into your house, confused
and disoriented, lost, as you find yourself now.
Adrift on wings that cannot hold them aloft—fizzing
with anger at the injustice of losing
themselves in a place they've never known
before.

Maybe this is how   civil war starts—
the first bullet shot, not   in patriotic fervor,
but in a flare of words: Stop.   No,
My son's body is   not yours to
destroy.

And you who caught a bat in a bedsheet,untangled
it under a new moon, waiting as it panted and clicked,
until it found its wings again. You who must hide
your quick anger from your son, lest he know
hate too soon—a nest hidden in the branches, its eggs
waiting to hatch some sunny afternoon not too long
from now.

Maybe this is how civil   war starts—
born sleepy-eyed and   hungry into
the bustle of the world, beak open wide for   what
its mother brings, until   it takes
flight, arcing , lofting on spirals of air,   far
from home.

Being Jewish in a Small Town

Lyn Lifshin

someone writes kike on
the blackboard and the
"k's" pull thru the
chalk, stick in my

plump pale thighs.
Even after the high
school burns down the
word is written in

the ashes. My under
pants' elastic snaps
on Main St because
I can't go to

Pilgrim Fellowship.
I'm the one Jewish girl
in town but the 4
Cohen brothers

want blond hair
blowing from their
car. They don't know
my black braids

smell of almond.
I wear my clothes
loose so no one
dreams who I am,

will never know
Hebrew, keep a
Christmas tree in
my drawer. In

the dark, my fingers
could be the menorah
that pulls you toward
honey in the snow

Black

Cathy Clay

Person of color—never; that umbrella covers many.
Negro had its day way before my time.
Colored waxed relevant on Grandma's lips;
She had lived, earned, and owned it.
But me, a child of the 70s, Black Arts, and hip-hop—
Black is my badge and sacred clarity.
I summon the word then things make sense.

African-American has provenance; consequently,
I was seventeen when the phrase broke ground.
There I was awaiting cap and gown, vying for colleges,
Casting wagers on womanhood. My cup ran over.
I stayed black.

Black is the truest color; where truth lies so does liberation.

Obscurity lets me smile from inside out, love who I want,
Rebuke who I don't, otherwise it lets me be. Like coal,
I cast embers for my blessings—cover curses with ash.

Night is absolute.

Loose ends vanish in the want of light. Cloaked in the shroud of
Ham, I maneuver undetected. Here I am, over, under, yonder.
Discernible upon invitation only.
After all, is black not a veil?

It is the truest color.
Where truth lies so does righteousness.
I need nothing else.

Brown Girl on the Tacoma Trolley

Carl Palmer

Not my daughter, my grand-daughter.
No, she's not adopted.
She speaks English, ask her.

Dear Claire (a letter poem)

Sharon A. Lewis

anchored in bygone
on an Atlantic barrier island
96th Street divided useight years September through June

eight years September through June
we skipped to a Lou
a Muffin Man on Drury Lane
played kickbaseball, sang "Frere Jacques"
giggled at Mrs. Walton's stilettos
learned ladyhood and how to keep houseeight

eight years July through September
from the back seat of my Mother's blue Bonneville
I scanned the borough's sidewalks, looking for you,
guessed the companions with whom
you somersaulted into the bay off your backyard wharf

too ashamed to fathom the ritual
summer sun's sweltering separation
you south, me north
our friendship as seasonal as greenheads
diamondback terrapins crossing the causeway
the drawbridge's sluggish risingmaybe the baggage was too heavy

maybe the baggage was too heavy
my speechless awareness of our differences
your ruby rosary bracelet
my grainy white leather Bible
your Coppertone, underwater hair
my bone screeching swim cap
your narrow feet, convex slender heels
mine two-toned, flat, plump like Aunt Emma's
my frozen ponytail
yours in perpetual swing

your saying once
"saliva arrives in the mouth
just before the volcano erupts"
years later in a university women's novels course
I would recall your biological expertise
liken us to a photo framed by Adrienne Richchildren

children, we could not know
(no one could would tell us)
later was coming
for both of us, same
race-time-for-sex-absolute-leave-taking
for each of us, different
a deluge of staggering blows
deferred furious awakenings
your traumas upsurging five times over

stay with me

from the still channel
I enter another inlet —
one void of collective tension and cultural rifts —
trawled west through the estuary to grasp

they tell me the bottle is how you cope
here is how for me

wherever you are
remember
we are neither urban nor rural
we are seaside
we are not castaways
we are starfish mollusks horseshoe crabs
becalmed by maritime rhythms

clutch your coastal passport, Claire
embrace our gentle hometown
whatever remains disquieting there
know that when we see each other again
you will reach for me and say in earnest:
"didn't we have fun?"

Firstborn

Vernita Hall

After a photograph of William E. B. Du Bois's son Burghardt Gomer Du Bois.
A white lace curtain partially overhangs the baby's head.

1899

My son, though Harvard-schooled, will see their blind
hatred still mock his budding brightness.
A Nigrah scholar. Thin smiles of forced politeness
will lock him tight behind the color-line.

Look, Gentle Reader: his perfect olive skin,
lith limbs, dark curls, questing blue-brown eyes,
legs crossed to guard his manhood. For behind
his back the laced white Veil descends.

In his baby voice I heard a future prophet.
But white doctors wouldn't treat a colored child They let—
liberty's a lie— diphtheria fester
At eighteen months his small soul self-sequestered

My son escaped Not dead not bound He's free
Must work Submission to such grief is slavery

In New Orleans

Alejandro Escude

It is the river
I recall, walking gingerly
down the plank
and to its shore
and putting one hand on it
(in it) and sensing
the history of bigotry.

Before boarding,
I made the black man
leap when I answered
a brusque "No!"
to his plead for a handout

and I recall thinking
how it was a strange leap
away from me.
Me? Who is anyone
to leap from me?

And it hurts, the no
I screamed out like a fool
making the other
tourists swing their heads
or shake them, though
maybe they didn't notice,
I can't remember.

But I do remember
the brown river
the wide, muggy river
and the smell of river

like pricey, wet leather.

Lingual Diversity

Carl Palmer

We share the bench
at a neighborhood park
by the court house
watch children play.

He says something, points
to a running, laughing boy,
probably his son,
about the same age as my daughter,
also running and laughing.

I point toward my little girl,
say the same thing in English
he most likely said in his language.

Like our children's laughter
we require no translation.

Point of View

Jeanne Lyet Gassman

Dear Officer, when you approach my son at 2:30 a.m. on a dark street,
Do you see

A young man with brown skin and brown eyes, a POC, a "person of color"?
Do you see the college graduate with a degree in criminal justice, the student
Who was on the Dean's list every semester, the one
Who, like you, works in law enforcement, but unlike you,
Who may work for the state or the city or the county, he
Is employed by the federal government, Homeland Security?

Do you see the boy
Who acolyted for our Episcopal Church, the man
Who mentored at-risk youth and volunteered at a homeless shelter, the child
Raised by white parents, the youngster
Who grew up
Upper-middleclass, attending one of the best public schools in the state?

Do you see a threat?

I warn my son "to be careful out there, to stay alert," and he reassures
Me: "Don't worry, Mom. I take off my uniform shirt as soon
As I leave work. I don't plan on being a target."
But why should he fear being a target?
No reassurance at all.

Do you see the other,
Someone unlike yourself,
And yet, so much like you
You cannot see?

My son and I, we talk sometimes about
The news, the racism, the violence, and I want
To tell him about past struggles, but
This world is not that world. This world is not

About Separate but Equal or sitting at the back of the bus or
Segregated bathrooms. There is no noble goal in this world for
Civil Rights or to end an unjust war. In this world, it is about
Us against Them, Liberal against Conservative, Islam against Christian,
Christian against Gay, Black against White, Police against Protester,
Citizen against Immigrant. In this
World, we fear the different, and foster
Unfocused rage.

My son and I, we talk, but
Our confusion leaves us
With no answers.

On a cold, blustery day my son dons
A hoodie to walk our dog to the park.
Neighbors do not avert their gaze or
Cross the street to avoid passing. They stop
To pet the dog, talk about the change in the weather, ask
About the family.

They know him. But you do not.

Dear Officer, when you stop my son at 2:30 a.m. for
A broken taillight, an illegal left turn, DWB,
Driving While Black,
For no reason at all, what do you see?

Do you see God's image in his African-American face?

Do you see a mother's fear for her son's safety?

Do you see?

The Artist's Grandmother's Carpet Hung on the Exhibit Wall

Kathrine Edgren

I see him
peeling carpet from wood floor, rolling it up,
with a plan to display this relic like a quilt,
top to ceiling, folded where it touches the floor.

This carpet-artist asks me to consider mundane objects
as art.

Dish-water beige, wearing dirt stains, remnants
of muddy feet, souvenirs of coming and going,
drinkers of coffee or tea. Perhaps a dog.

Carpet as detritus, carpet as life-witness.
Well-worn rug, well-worn grandmother,
who may have tried to clean it,
or maybe carpet stains were the least of her concerns.

There to keep her feet from touching cold,
for softening the jar, preventing a hard slip and fall.

He liked to visit Grandmother's house.
The carpet means home,
and he wants to preserve some piece of it, or

he never noticed the carpet
until she died, spending his attention on the woman herself, or

he neglected to visit at all,
and didn't see the carpet until it
was all that was left.

The carpet is loneliness.
The carpet is the artist's regret,
gray sky, horizon of sadness.

The artist was Rodney McMillian, and his art work, "Untitled." The exhibit was called 30 Americans, and was meant to be an eye-opener on the black experience. At the Detroit Institute of the Arts, January 2016.

The disappeared

Janette Schafer

Jorge was my dad's younger brother. In an old picture I am dressed as a clown for *Carnival* in Venezuela, holding onto tio while we are both smiling. He became a *los desaparecidos* in his early twenties, but he was so aloof it is hard to say exactly when we lost him. Hugo Chavez, he liked to take sons away from mothers, brothers away from sisters, husbands from wives, uncles from little girls. After twenty years, Jorge meets a cousin in a market in Caracas as he shops for *platanos* and *pabellon* as if he had been living there all along. He cannot tell her where he has been. He says he will find her again but artificial lights and large crowds make him sad and crazy. His eyes are corn husks, skin shucked wheat. He is not returned so much as transformed, a reverse chrysalis, *mariposa* yielding to the caterpillar crawling on the belly. *Los desaparecidos*, they are never supposed to come back.

There will not be unity

Keri L. Withington

I did not choose this skin.
I could scrub myself pink/raw
but the white would not wash off
Guilt sticks like the freckles my little
sister tried to wash off in our
toddlerhood baths, convinced
I was dirty

Until my country does our dirty work
recognizes that the bedrock of American
Democracy is the attempted physical and cultural genocide
of indigenous peoples, we will not be able to truly advance How
can we achieve unity with anyone until all
Americans are included
at the table

Their DNA is embedded in our cities
the river names we pronounce unthinkingly
The landscape still remembers: Appalachian foothills,
Dogwood trees, rhododendrons ready
to teach us what it means
to be human

A Lesson in Silence

Jesus Antonio Esparza

My hand a sickle at the base of a paper cup, circles
small cricket leaps when mother tells me
tia Lety passed. Her face a bronze stain against

the screen door tries to hold something broken inside
rushes me into deep blue jeans, dress shoes too big
for my feet, plaid collar shirt with a bolo tie. Her hand

darkened by a procession of black pearls, I know
where we're going today. Breathe in a highway hum
dressed in a suit appropriate for the dead, my arm

stretches across plastic below the window of the car,
chin resting on my hand, I watch tree lines fill my
window, an ocean flip-book through rooftops. The flag

of Mexico craters a geyser into the sky, a wing
trying to slap its way out of the overcast unraveling
in the glare. My mother's eyes in the rear view mirror

find themselves struggling to catch my daydream,
the way I ambushed crickets in a paper cup, my ear
pressed close listening for silence as I tapped my index

on the top. Under her breath my mother whispers
a prayer that floats toward the windshield— weighted
stillness pushed against the glass. Her eyes

find me again, I knew there was nothing
I could say, only hope that when the crickets
were freed they would find their way home.

In the Name of the Father

Jesus Antonio Esparza

Amid a humid summer, I was given a name.
My language hid from its own voice. At 6 I lost my name.

> My *new name*, school officials deemed more appropriate,
> easier to say they would say. An American name.

In Mexico, an entire country is handed down
to their children. Hyphens become the link between a name.

> The umbilical strangled my son's neck as it rained,
> sang him the one lullaby I know, and gave him my name.

My mother has told me that my father loves me.
But the last time he called, he couldn't even say my name.

> *Jesus* is usually confused with the almighty.
> He's really only a poet, holding onto a name.

What Thirst Looks Like

Jesus Antonio Esparza

My son's first word   *aqua*, what thirst
looked like to a eight month old. He would

point to the refrigerator tap his mouth *aqua*.
My first valentine's card, I wrote

for my grandmother In Spanish, she refused
to learn English even after crossing

a chalk line that was the border. Before
the drones, before the wars, rocks against

windshields, gunshots to ribcage, no water
in the valley. She ended most evenings

with a Coors Light a little lime, and a
tortilla de maiz doradita with a hint of butter,

before breathing a soft prayer
into a small photo of San Cristóbal Magallenes Jara.

My son would reach—

for my glass on the coffee table aqua.
I handed the card to my grandmother,

she read and whispered in my ear
to never let go,

por que la lengua mijo,
nadie te puede quitar. My son

from the back seat would push his hand
against the glass, an ocean filling

the window aqua.

A Prayer Through White Noise

Jesus Antonio Esparza

When John F. Kennedy was assassinated
mi abuela had been in el norte for four days.

She arrived on 13th street, three daughters
one that still couldn't tie her own shoes. No television,

a hand held radio with a broken antenna tuned
to one station of faint low resolution Baptist prayers

hollered through white noise. My abuela is Catholic,
finding refuge in a Jesus that can roll his R's. She held

a rosary near her chest, radio on the yellow-tiled kitchen
counter while she listened. Although she didn't understand,

she believed this brought her closer to accepting
all the billboards, missing children on cartons — *Amereeqa*,

where the screen doors locked behind her. That morning,
her two oldest daughters came home with a gallon of milk,

oceans filling the bottom of their eyes, questions of why
the lady at the Mini-mart couldn't remove her hand

from the television, choking with each breath. Reports
static of a bullet entering then exiting the back of a skull.

Rolling the R

Jesus Antonio Esparza

I learned to speak English
watching Tom and Jerry, stand up

bass lines sprinting into the mouse
hole, violins swatting the tail.

Señora Kelly never liked my accent,
told me I colored the wrong intersection

bubble. Slowed down her speech, red
goes *here* pointing, tapping the circle. I still

don't know when to stop sometimes. *Si dios
quiere* me dice mi abuela, you will learn to unfold

the ere from the R's, level the squiggly line
above the N. Sunday morning I would crash—

in front of the television, 7:30 channel 13
milk tipping from the spoon, my father showered

and sang another corrido that fingered along
the medicine cabinet mirror. Atop the kitchen

table Jerry stuffed an iron into a meringue pie,
Tom thumbing the upright, singing the blues.

White Barbie

Sean Johnson

Handing me a blonde haired, blue-eyed Barbie
in Ross Department Store,
my niece sweetly asks, "Can I have this?"

This suburban daughter only sees a doll.
She's from Kindles and hashtags,
Justice stores and diversity.
I'm from Reaganomics and The Cosby Show.
We're both post-civil rights and pre-Armageddon,
but I've been around long enough to see racism become
the "nothing new under the sun."
And so I tell her,

You may not have that doll.
Though she looks like many of your friends,
she will one day become the enemy of your self-esteem.
White Barbie's figure
was precast by European ideals of perfection,
but your Coke bottle/
top heavy/
thick hipped/
bow legged/
big booty was precast by God.
Her perfectly painted on face
could not come close to the rich
golden red undertones in your Africa,
nor could her synthetic shell
ever reflect the perfection in your melanin.

Her silky locks will never capture the rage against gravity
in your kinky curls as they rise from nappy roots.
Her artificial frame won't have enough give in the hips
to reconstruct the breadth of your Ohio
or imitate that wobble in your walk.

Furthermore, White Barbie may sell out
but she will never have to sell out,
nor will she work twice as hard for half of her dream house.
She will come with accessories
in addition to the privileges of her white skin.

Her Ken won't be caged unjustly and seen in segments
through the crisscross of security glass.
His hands will always be up
with no afterthoughts for "Don't shoot."
He won't have to remind America that his life matters.

White Barbie bears no resemblance to your history.
Her arms have never bent to pick cotton.
Her belly never swelled with Panther cubs.
Her knees were not made to bend without breaking.
Her legs won't ever step wide enough
to cover the distance between broken dreams.
Her feet could not walk
an Underground Railroad in your shoes.

You cannot have a White Barbie.
She does not acknowledge your mind's radiance nor
will she confess that she's been clutching
the shadows of your Cleopatra
since she first set foot on your continent.
All White Barbie's ever wanted to be was you,
and because she could not achieve it,
she settled for being plastic.

Buttonwillows

Elaine Shea

A huge field of gray seed onions stood tall.
I couldn't see anything
beyond their sheer beauty
and cloudy mist rising
above flower hats
waiting to be topped.

Burlap bags resting on the soil
are brown and wrinkled like
migrant farm workers
who pick in rainy fields
surrounded by bags of onions
spilling onto wet ground
ready for packing.

Concrete Cornfields

TOO BLACK

I'm from the breeding grounds of the Klan
The land
where trife lives
Where life is
an identity crisis
Where white kids
rock du rags and sag
at the same time while they fly a confederate flag

Where you can be their nigger or their nigga'
Depending on how you want to figure
And it ain't just black and white
No
Here life is a colorful
self-destructible picture
It only depends on how you want to frame it

Yet we claim it's
'just entertainment'
while appropriating language
and culture
to which we have absolutely no exposure

So there's 'No Limits'
Who are you?
A souljah?
A trapper?
An MC?
An east or west coast rapper?
A backpacker?
Because if you don't play your hand correctly
You can directly
get got
by the cross-cultural mad hatter

With illusions ooozin' from the tip of your brim
Broke rockin' a fitted
Thinking somehow because you listen
to Jay Z you can get it just like him
"Nigga are you crazy?"

See cats be delirious
We don't know what time period we in
This is Indiana
The state of confusion
The southern state of the north
This place was built off course
Meaning you can't ever expect it to find it's right path
A melting pot
Poisoned to rot
Stewing and brewing a class
of niggers and white trash

We're fed our roles early
We're presumed from the womb to be typecast
Groomed to play our parts
This is where life imitates art
So welcome to the multicultural minstrel show
Where black guys are like white guys
baptized in black dye
So the consequence is to Shuck N Jive
Becomes synonymous with black pride

Maybe that's why yoloism is the new religion
Because we're only livin' once to die
My brother became blessed in through prison
to get is body and soul sanctified
Still I can't deny
that both of our minds are institutionalized
This is a fact that I used to deny
Until I opened my eyes and realized
that I dwell in a bottomless nocuous hell

Yet they say hell is a state of mind
So me over thinkin' is a demon

Which explains the reason
why I'm breathin' and weezin'
To ex-hell
Escaping a land reeking of that dead flesh smell
Swimming through a sewer of old Hoosier manure
Where underneath this manhole
Life becomes too difficult for the bulk to handle

Race and class go toe-to-toe
Any middle class existence gets overthrown
By a system of post-apocalyptic capitalism
Factory jobs got robbed
Opportunities stolen
Dreams got lifted

Now they're handling me a bible
with needles and scriptures
Saying in order to take away the pain
shoot up your veins with religious traditions
Now I'm seeing track marks on Christians
Sorry my nigga but I must be born a sinner
Because when it comes to this nonsense
I lack conviction

Still with all the religious contradictions
And racial tensions
This is the side in which I reside
Despite the social ills that persist
This is a place where hope and faith can still exist
Yes, sometimes I can be a borderline atheist
Yet, when it comes to the state of Indiana
From these cornfields to our concrete
I pray for this

Scripts

The Oreo Complex

Quintessa Knight

Time

- Modern Day

Place

- Therapist's office

Characters

- Allison
- Holden
- Kiara
- Eric
- Therapist
- Three Party-goers

THERAPIST

I've got to say I was surprised when you scheduled me. I haven't seen you in a while. So how have you been?

KIARA

I'm fine…. well…not fine. Doesn't it feel weird for a person to say they're fine when they're in their therapist's office? It's like going to the doctor with a broken leg and he asks how you're doing. Clearly something's wrong or I wouldn't be here.

THERAPIST

You're right. I'm sorry I asked.

KIARA

No, no

(sigh)

I didn't mean to sound rude. I'm sorry…I've just been thinking a lot about…
people. You know? Our human nature and how we deal with things.

THERAPIST

Anything in particular that you're dealing with, Kiara?

KIARA

So, I went to my best friend's engagement party this weekend. Which is really
important not just because I'm her maid of honor but we haven't seen each
other since high school.

THERAPIST

Four years is a long time. You must have been excited.

KIARA

I was…anxious. I mean it's been a long time and I realized a lot of things
might have changed. See, Allison's kind of a free spirit. She could literally roll a
dice and let it decide where she lives for the next three years and she'd be
perfectly fine if she ended up in a monastery in Tibet getting the first foreign
word she saw permanently etched into her skin.

THERAPIST

Wow. That's quite a description.

KIARA

Yeah, but don't get me wrong though she's one of my biggest inspirations.
She does what she wants to and says what she wants to and I've always kind of
envied that.

THERAPIST

And you?

KIARA

Me? I think…a lot. I have to plan out what I'm going to say before I even leave the house. I'm careful and it's fine, I've accepted it. But something bugged me the whole while leading up to the bridal shower and I couldn't put my finger on what exactly it was.

THERAPIST

Is that what you're here to discuss?

KIARA

Yeah but it's bigger than that see in high school I was kind of a square. I wasn't "black enough" for the kids on my block and I wasn't bothered enough to figure out what that meant so Allison and I bonded over stuff like anime and alternative rock. When we graduated, I worked three jobs to get into an HBCU out of state and she was using her college fund to explore the world.

THERAPIST

Did that upset you?

KIARA

What?

THERAPIST

Did it upset you that Allison was better-off than you were?

KIARA

Funny phrase…better-off…well-off. White people don't like to say rich, do they?

THERAPIST

You didn't answer the question.

KIARA

No. It doesn't bother me that my best friend was rich. It bothered me that my best friend complained while being rich. In the amount of time it took me to save up for college she'd already owned three different luxury vehicles but she was still upset because neither of them were what she'd asked for.

THERAPIST

How'd that make you feel?

KIARA

How did that make me

(short laugh)

...okay here's how I felt. You know that scene from Titanic where Rose and Jack are in the ocean and she's floating on this piece of bed and she's like "I'm so cold, Jack" meanwhile Leonardo DiCaprio's character is in the fucking water, literally living in hypothermia as he takes his last dying breath.

THERAPIST

Mmhmm...

KIARA

Well, that's how I fucking felt. Constantly there to encourage this person they're going to be fine meanwhile I'm cold and I'm drowning. Only I hadn't got that feeling in a really long time... until the bridal shower.

THERAPIST

Well, let's take it back a little bit. Tell me about what happened after you went to college? You said you didn't have many black friends...do you think that affected your experience at a black college?

KIARA

Well, yeah I changed. I grew up in this neighborhood where I wasn't black enough for black people but I was still too black for white people. You know what they call people like me? An oreo. White on the inside, black on the outside. But then I get to this school and I think if I can make it through four years of being an outcast there certainly I can do it here.

THERAPIST

Is that how it was for you?

KIARA

No. Not at all. The ironic thing about being at a school with primarily black people is you stop being a black writer or a black nerd. You're just a writer and you're just a nerd. I didn't have to suppress one half of myself and it felt…good. I stopped dating certain guys-

THERAPIST

White guys?

KIARA

No, not white guys. I stopped dating any guy that felt the need to say shit like "Kiara you're the darkest girl I've ever dated" or "I don't think you should wear braids when you meet my parents." Doesn't matter whether his name was Thad, Tyrell or Juan…I stopped.

THERAPIST

Continue.

KIARA

Because I started to have an opinion. A political opinion, an ethical opinion. An…ethnic opinion.

THERAPIST

Did Allison understand your views?

KIARA

You know everyone is always telling me how lucky I am to still have the same best friend I had in high school. But I don't know my best friend from high school. I'm afraid to.

THERAPIST

Okay, well go ahead and tell me about the bridal shower.

(KIARA gets up and a white sheet is spread across the therapist desk, she sits and begins to tell her story. NOTE: KIARA often freezes the situation to speak with her THERAPIST)

KIARA

(Deep sigh)

Alright so I get there and the venue is huge…obviously. Her parents paid for the whole thing. All the cups have customized monograms of the bride and groom's names. This is not the same emo chick who wore heavy eyeliner and a septum piercing. And there's kind of this sigh of relief like whew! I'm not the only one who's changed. Well anyways, I'm sitting at this table full of girls, oh fuck, I forget their names but they had way too many Y's in each of them and I'm pretty sure more than one of their middle names was Lynn, Leigh or Marie. And we're all just chatting it up when I realized what it was that was so weird.

THERAPIST

What was it?

KIARA

I was the only black person there. And there had to be about fifty people there. I felt like I was in a Jordan Peele psychological thriller. I was suddenly just hyper aware of everything. My natural hair, my skin, the way people pronounced my name, the things they said…

THERAPIST

What'd they say?

KIARA

They'd say things like…

GUEST #1

So, you're the black writer we've heard so much about. Here she is, the maid of honor, Kara!

KIARA

Actually, it's —

GUEST #2

Yes, I read some of your work. Sooo well-written!

KIARA

Thanks?

GUEST #3

Didn't you go to Howard? I have a friend named Jamal there. Do you know him?

KIARA

Why should I?

GUEST #1

(Awkwardly)

Girl your dress is so on fleek! When we get to the reception you gotta teach me how to twerk, okay?

KIARA

But the conversations I wasn't invited in to were far worse...

GUEST #2

I just think they're being oversensitive, if they don't like this country they can always go back.

KIARA

Sure, when does the next slave ship leave?

GUEST #3

What's equal about an NAACP? If you ask me there should be a WAACP.

KIARA

I was afraid to ask what he thought the "N" stood for?

GUEST #1

I personally would feel a lot safer if he did build the wall.

KIARA

They vacation in Cancun every summer.

THERAPIST

And how did you respond to all of that?

KIARA

It's one thing to be the only black woman in the room but to be the angry black woman in the room

(she gives the audience a look)

By the third Danielle Bregoli impersonation I was all but ready to run out the door.

THERAPIST

Well it seems like they meant well.

KIARA

Well duh, even racist mean well

THERAPIST

Is that what they were to you? Racist?

KIARA

All white people are racist.

THERAPIST

Excuse me?

KIARA

It's possible to have good intentions and still be racist.

THERAPIST

Can you elaborate?

KIARA

Your intentions could be to be inclusive but they can still be racist. Or maybe your intentions were to be funny, it can still be racist.

THERAPIST

Well if they're all racist then why even question what Allison was.

KIARA

Well I knew then that she was prejudiced, you can't just invite over fifty white people and one black person to a gathering without making a statement no matter how great your intentions may be but I needed to know how prejudiced. Was she Trump or was she Clinton? Did she even vote? All Lives Matter?

THERAPIST

Did you find out?

KIARA

I'm getting there...okay so I'm lingering by the door when...

ERIC

Hey! You must be Kiara, the maid of honor? I'm Eric.

KIARA

Nice to meet you, you might be the first person here to call me that.

ERIC

Good. It only took hoping into five other conversations before I finally caught it.

KIARA

What were they calling me?

ERIC

The black bridesmaid, that black girl, the overdressed waitress–

KIARA

OK, we're done here.

ERIC

(laughs)

No, no, I'm kidding. I made up that last one.

KIARA

Glad to see at least one of us is comfortable.

ERIC

The last thing I came over here to do was make you feel more uncomfortable. I apologize.

KIARA

Exactly what did you come over here to do?

ERIC

To give you some company. Halt your attempts at an easy escape.

KIARA

We're not that acquainted yet.

ERIC

Look I get it. The situation sucks but I know Allison wants you here.

KIARA

How do you know wha– ...wait...Eric...Eric, the best man?

ERIC

At your service.

KIARA

Allison told me about you. You're–

ERIC

The gay best friend?

KIARA

I was going to say the blunt one.

ERIC

Seems to be the closest thing we have in common tonight.

KIARA

Look, it was one time in college but I'm not–

ERIC

No, dear. I meant we're the token friends. We're the ones that keep our conservative friends looking a little less...bland, you know. The Get Out of Jail Free card when someone wants to say something really fucked up.

KIARA

Wow.

ERIC

You're damn right wow. I hadn't heard from Holden in two years when he invited me to be in the wedding.

KIARA

Are you serious?

ERIC

He didn't take it too well when I came out of the closet.

KIARA

That bad?

ERIC

If it were up to him he would have dumped some luggage on top to keep me in there.

KIARA

But you still showed up?

ERIC

You still showed up.

KIARA

Human nature, I guess.

ERIC

We want people to treat us as well as we treat them.

KIARA

I'm not anyone's token...I don't want to be–

ERIC

Well hun, you should have thought about that before you RSVP'd but today you're the chili pepper garnish that makes the white rice look more ethnic.

KIARA

What does that make you?

ERIC

(with thought)

Me? I'm the meatless vegan option here to represent the alternative lifestyle.

KIARA

(laughs)

How can you make a joke about all of this?

ERIC

(shrugs)

If you're laughing they're comfortable.

KIARA

Yeah but if you're angry they're paying attention.

ERIC

What kind of attention? Mm...don't answer that yet, the unseasoned chicken is ready.

(ALLISON and HOLDEN enter slightly tipsy)

Well hello, lovebirds!

ALLISON

We've been looking all over for you guys!

HOLDEN

We were about to make a toast.

(ERIC gets up to leave)

ALLISON

Eric, where do you think you're going?

ERIC

I'll be back, I don't have enough vodka for this.

HOLDEN

(to Allison)

He's full of jokes.

Let me get everyone's attention. I'd like to propose a toast. To the maid of honor and the best man.

ALLISON

I'll start with you, Kiara. You've been such an amazing friend to me for so long and I'm so glad you're a part of my wedding. I don't think either one of us saw this day coming but I'm so happy you're a part of it. Come over here! Don't be shy!

(ALLISON playfully tugs KIARA's arm)

I need everyone to see who you are. My homie, my sister, my nigga…

(KIARA pulls her arm away.)

KIARA

Excuse me?! What did you call me? Actually no, don't repeat it.

ALLISON

Kiara, I didn't mean it like that!

KIARA

Well how the hell else could you have meant it! Have you looked around, Allison?! Have you noticed something kind of...off?

ALLISON

(whispers)

Kiara, you're making a scene!

KIARA

If this is a scene then, honey you're the star. How does it feel? Does it feel uncomfortable? Embarrassing? Does it feel like everyone's eyes are on you? Judging you heavily...

ALLISON

KIARA! This is not the time —

KIARA

Oh, it's not the time for me to talk about it but it was the time for you to say it?

ALLISON

You're overreacting!

KIARA

I...

THERAPIST

Well...

KIARA

Well what?

THERAPIST

You stopped.

KIARA

That's not what happened.

THERAPIST

Then how did you react?

KIARA

I didn't.

THERAPIST

Kiara, you said something upsetting happened at the shower, something confrontational that caused you to question your human nature. You didn't get mad? Upset? Lash out at Allison?

KIARA

I wanted too.

THERAPIST

Well why not? You've spent this whole time telling me you were offended. There's got to be some reason you didn't say anything?

KIARA

That was why. It would have been expected of me and I didn't want to do what was expected of me.

THERAPIST

Well something had to happen next.

KIARA

I thanked her for inviting me. They laughed and I drank. They spoke some more and I drank some more. I drank the rest of that night until I drowned myself in the idea that it never even happened. That I had overreacted. I told myself if Eric could show up and play it cool that I could too.

THERAPIST

But you weren't —

KIARA

I was cold and I was drowning. In the middle of a joyous occasion surrounded by strangers that wouldn't understand, or at least wouldn't like to try. I was well spoken, polite, and presentable to them. However, on the inside I was overthinking every word, every action of the things I said or didn't say. And I don't know who I was in that room that night but I wasn't that girl that I graduated as. Being there I didn't feel black and when I left I wasn't proud. I wasn't white. Who was I? Why didn't I speak up

Contributors

Shanita Bigelow
Shanita Bigelow is originally from North Carolina. She currently resides in Chicago, where she is pursuing her doctorate in education.

TOO BLACK
TOO BLACK is a spoken word poet, public speaker, activist and educator based in Indianapolis, IN. The name TOO BLACK developed as a challenge to society on the perceptions of blackness and humanity especially in the United States. Influenced by a wide variety of artists and historical figures – from Malcolm X to Gore Vidal, from George Carlin to Audre Lorde – TOO BLACK fuses these multiple perspectives, his life exploration and passionate performance bringing them to life on the stage. His working dialogue draws from personal experiences, historical and current events and the culture of Hip Hop in which he was born. He describes his performance as a "conversation" in which he talks with his audiences and connects their shared experiences. TOO BLACK recently was awarded the Indy Art Council's Beckmann Fellowship. Overall, TOO BLACK performs poetry professionally around the world from Princeton to South Africa.

Cathy Clay
My name is Cathy Clay, and I am a Houston, Texas native. I earned a bachelor's degree in Creative Writing from the University of Houston (1997) and a master's in English from Texas Southern University (2008). My scholarly reviews have been published in the *Facts on File: Companion to the World Novel* published by Columbia University Press (2007) and my short stories have been featured in literary journals. My debut novel, *Agatta*, was published in 2010. Currently my short stories, "Cecil" and "The Earrings," appear in *Eclectically Criminal* and *Eclectically Cosmic* respectively, both Inklings Publications. My poem, "Hiss", was published by *Rat's Ass Review* (2017) in their *Such an Ugly Time* collection.

Katherine Edgren
Katherine Edgren grew up in Grand Rapids, Michigan. She was first published in 1967 at the age of seventeen under her maiden name: Kathy Kool. She began to write more seriously in 2004, and was awarded first place in the *Writer's*

Digest non-rhyming poetry contest, and appeared in The Year's Best Writing in 2005. She has been published in the *Christian Science Monitor*, as well as various journals including the *Birmingham Poetry Review*, *Barbaric Yawp*, *Main Channel Voices*, *Oracle*, *Bear Creek Haiku*, the *Coe Review*, and the *Evening Street Review*. Katherine served three terms as a City Councilmember in Ann Arbor, Michigan, raised money for the ACLU, and worked as a project manager on research and intervention projects in Detroit addressing asthma and air quality. She has worked with adults with serious mental illnesses, with ex-offenders, and with college students. She is now retired and lives in Dexter, Michigan. Katherine Edgren's book *The Grain Beneath the Gloss*, published by Finishing Line Press, will be available in September. She also has two chapbooks: *Long Division* and *Transports*. She has been working on a blog about poetry and photography and will soon open it to the public.

Alejandro Escudé

Alejandro Escudé's first book of poems, *My Earthbound Eye*, was published in September 2013. He holds a master's degree in creative writing from UC Davis and teaches English. Originally from Argentina, Alejandro lives in Los Angeles with his wife and two children.

Jesus A Esparza

Chicano Americano poet Jesus Antonio Esparza received his BA in Chicana/o Studies, and MFA from San Diego State University. Here, he honed his skills as once Hip Hop artist that was the creative backbone of two full length albums, and one international selling single. Soon after, Esparza translated his music experience and stage presence into performance poet, where he became a key contributor in the nascent stage of a community based artist space in San Diego, California. Esparza's work is a direct reflection of an upbringing within a rough, predominantly Latino neighborhood, which thrust him onto the cusp of everything from gang activity to drug use. In addition, Esparza explores navigating the "American" landscape within an ever present struggle of identity between his Mexican heritage, and American traditions. While at SDSU, Esparza's work landed him a Best New Poet nomination from the faculty. His most recent work has been published by Locked Horn Press.

Beverly Faragasso

I think of myself as a housewife who tries to tell stories on paper. I often write about illness both from the perspective of survivors and caregivers, giving "voice" to those who will probably never get a chance to tell their own stories. I do not write regularly or with a well laid out schedule. My husband struggles with Parkinson's Disease, a chronic illness, and my ninety-four year old widowed father, although living independently, needs me to go with him to doctors' appointments and sometimes just to be present in his life. Because of this, I write on the periphery of our three lives — before sunrise, in waiting rooms, between.

Jeanne Lyet Gassman

Jeanne Lyet Gassman's first novel, *Blood of a Stone* (Tuscany Press), received a 2015 Independent Publisher's Book Award (bronze) in the national category of religious fiction. Additional awards include fellowships from Ragdale and the Arizona Commission on the Arts. Her shorter work has been nominated for a Pushcart and Best Small Fictions and has appeared or is forthcoming in *Bosque Press, Hippocampus, The Manifest-Station, Red Savina Review,* and *Literary Mama,* among many others. Her short story, "Sweet Dirty Love," was recently published in the anthology, *Debris & Detrius: The Lesser Greek Gods Running Amok.* Learn more about Jeanne at her website: www.jeannelyetgassman.com

Vernita Hall

A Rosemont College MFA, Vertina Hall placed second in *American Literary Review*'s Creative Nonfiction Contest' as a finalist for the *Cutthroat* Barry Lopez Nonfiction, *Rita Dove, Paumanok,* and *Atlanta Review* Poetry Awards; a semi-finalist in the *Naugatuck River Review* Narrative Poetry Contest and *Ruminate*'s VanderMey Nonfiction Prize, the Hitchhiking Robat Learns About Philadelphians won the 2016 Moonstone chapbook Contest (judge Afaa Michael Weaver). She serves on the poetry review board of *Philadelphia Stories.* Poetry and essays appears or are forthcoming in *Atlanta Review, Philadelphia Stories, Referential, Mezzo Cammin, Whirlwind, Canary, African American Review, Snapdragon,* anthology *Forgotten Women* (Grayson Books), and five other anthologies.

Lynn Casteel Harper

Lynn Casteel Harper's work has appeared in *North American Review, Kenyon Review Online, Catapult, New Delta Review,* The Huffington Post, *Tiferet, So to Speak, CALYX, Big Muddy, Journal of Religion and Abuse,* and elsewhere. She received the *New Delta Review*'s 2013 Nonfiction Prize and was named runner-up for the Torch Prize (2016). Originally from southeastern Missouri, she lives in New York City where she on staff at The Riverside Church as the minister with older adults. She is currently completing a book of essays, *When I Have Dementia*, which received a Barbara Deming Fund grant for women writers.

D.A. Hosek

D. A. Hosek's writing has appeared in *Westerly*, *Meniscus*, *The Southampton Review* and elsewhere. His story, "Our Lady of the Freeway" won the 2016 Headlands Prize. He earned an MFA in fiction from the University of Tampa. He lives and writes in Oak Park, IL and spends his days as an insignificant cog in the machinery of corporate America.

Sean Johnson

Sean Johnson is a teacher by trade but enjoys writing and has starred in several local plays. Her work has appeared in *Tiger's Eye*, *Riversongs*, *Houston Poetry Anthology*, *Sierra Nevada Review*, *Sanskrit*, *Third Wednesday*, and other journals. In Spring 2017, she will be releasing her first full length anthology of poetry entitled *All My Heroes Were Assassinated*. Sean resides in Houston, Texas with her beloved dog, Bruce Leroy.

Quintessa Knight

Quintessa Knight is a graduate of Georgia Southern University with a Bachelor of Arts in Theatre and a minor in Film. She now resides in Savannah, Georgia where she enjoys writing short plays and stories that reflect social issues. Knight's work is often provoked by real life events centered around racial identity. Her first short story, "Honeysuckle Prince", was awarded the AWP Intro Journals Award in 2017 and is published in *Hayden's Ferry Review*. When she's not writing, her other hobbies include acting, drawing and procrastination over Netflix with her cat.

Sharon A. Lewis

Sharon A. Lewis, is a retired Professor Emerita/English from Montclair State University. There, she taught African American women's literature, women prose writers, and introduction to literary theory. Her research interests are the literary intersections of capitalism, race and gender and environmental thought in Black women's novels.

Lyn Lifshin

Lyn Lifshin has published over 130 books and chapbooks including 3 from Black Press: *Cold Comfort*, *Before it's Light*, and *Another Woman who Looks Like Me*. Recent books include: *Secretariat: The Red Freak, The Miracle*; *Knife*

Edge & Absinthe: the Tango Poems. Malala; A Girl Goes into the Woods; Femme Eterna; Little Dancer: the Degas Poems and alivelikealoadedgun. She edited 3 anthologies: *Tangled vines, Lips Unsealed; Ariadne's Thread.* Her website: www: lynlifshin.com

Dheepa R. Maturi

Dheepa R. Maturi is the director of an education grant program in Indianapolis and a graduate of the University of Michigan (A.B. English Literature) and the University of Chicago (J.D.). Her work has appeared (or is forthcoming) in *Brevity, Every Day Poems, Tweetspeak Poetry, A Tea Reader, Mothers Always Write, Here Comes Everyone, Flying Island, Branches, Corium,* and *The Indianapolis Review.* Her short story "Three Days" was a finalist in the Tiferet 2017 Writing Contest. www.DheepaRMaturi.com

Carl Palmer

Carl "Papa" Palmer of Old Mill Road in Ridgeway, VA now lives in University Place, WA. He is retired military, retired FAA and now just plain retired without wristwatch or alarm clock. MOTTO: Long Weekends Forever.

Kristen Mai Pham

Kristen Mai Pham's love for writing began in high school. She is passionate about sharing her moving, uplifting stories of inspiration, healing, hope, refugee identity, happiness, and fulfillment. One day, she hopes that her words will mend the heart, instill love, forge togetherness, incite gratitude, champion the human spirit, soothe wounded souls, and inspire acts of kindness. Kristen is a two-time contributor to the iconic *Chicken Soup for the Soul* book series. She divides her time between authoring short stories, screenwriting, and blogging. She has completed several heartwarming screenplays and is in discussions with multiple production companies. Her book, *From Refugee to Writer,* is targeted for release by September of 2018.

Rebecca Redshaw

Rebecca Redshaw is an author and playwright who lives in the Pacific Northwest. In addition to extensive articles and short stories published in national newspapers and magazines, she has self-published a novella, *Dear Jennifer* as well as *SOFA CINEMA: An Easy Guide to DVDs, Vol. 1*– a compilation of her published DVD critiques. A theatrical adaptation of *Dear Jennifer* and *FOUR WOMEN,* an original play, have been produced in the United States and Canada. She was awarded First Prize in the 2009 Lakeview

Literary Review for her short story, "Somebody Special". In 2016, she was awarded third prize in the Soul-Making Keats Contest for her short story, "Mrs. C". Currently, she is at work on her fourth novel and eighth play. A complete literary vitae can be accessed at www.rebeccaredshaw.com.

Luisa Kay Reyes

Luisa Kay Reyes has had pieces featured in the *Fire In Machines*, Hofstra University's *The Windmill, Halcyon Days, Fellowship of the King, Enchanted Conversation: A Fairy Tale Magazine*, the *Route – 7 – Review, The Foliate Oak, The Eastern Iowa Review*, and other literary magazines. Her piece, "Thank You", is the winner of the April 2017 memoir contest of "The Dead Mule School Of Southern Literature." And her Christmas poem was a first place winner in the 16th Annual Stark County District Library Poetry Contest. Additionally, her essay "My Border Crossing" has just been nominated for the Pushcart Prize by the Port Yonder Press.

Janette Schafer

Janette Schafer is a playwright, poet, and opera singer from Pittsburgh, Pennsylvania. A Venezuelan native, she moved to the United States at the age of three. She is a 2017 winner of the Maenad Fellowship in writing through Chatham University. Her play 'northeastsouthwest' a collaborative writing experiment with five other playwrights debuted at the 2016 Pittsburgh Fringe Festival, winning the Spirit of the Fringe Award. Some upcoming and recent publications include: The Woman, Inc., Eyedrum Periodically, Nasty Women and Bad Hombres, BE Literary Journal.

Heather Schroeder

I am an assistant professor of English at Pellissippi State Community College in Knoxville, Tennessee. I am an essayist, fiction writer, and poet. My nonfiction book *A Reader's Guide to Marjane Satrapi's 'Persepolis'* was released by Enslow Publishing in January 2010, and my fiction, poetry and essays have appeared in *Southern Indiana Review*, bornmagazine.com, *Iron Horse Literary Review, Wisconsin People and Ideas, Beloit Fiction Journal, The Virginia Quarterly Review*, and *The Cream City Review*. I received my MFA from the University of Wisconsin-Madison in 2006.

Elaine Shea

Elaine Dugas Shea grew up by the ocean, but has lived in Missoula, Montana since 1972. Beginning as a "Vista" Volunteer and Civil Rights Worker in

Atlanta, Georgia, 1966, she went on to serve American Indian, Alaska Native and Migrant & Seasonal Farmworker children & families as a national Head Start Grantee Specialist. In addition to capturing details about her travels, Elaine's writing evolved into poetry about inequality, the struggles of the human condition, nature, dreams and images which pass through her sleep refusing to be ignored. Her poems were featured in diverse national and regional anthologies including *Camas, Poems Across the Big Sky II, Cirque, Cowboy Poetry Press, Haight Ashbury Literary Journal, Hot Air Quarterly, Reverie, South Dakota Review, Spillway, Third Wednesday,* When Last on the Mountain and elsewhere. Her poetry collection, "Dream Transfer and Wander" published January 2017, is available at Amazon.com. Elaine, chickadeepc@gmail.com, is the lucky grandmother of Arthur, Walter and Jasmine.

Samuel Son

Samuel Son is a columnist at *North State Journal* and *Presbyterian Outlook.* a regular contributor at *Sojourner, Mockingbird,* and others. His poems and short stories have been published or forthcoming at *Cultural Weekly, Cleaver Magazine,* and others. www.sonsamuel.com.

Keri L. Withington

Keri Withington is a parent, educator, poet, and activist. Her poetry has appeared in numerous journals and anthologies, recently including *Blue Fifth Review, New Plains Review,* and *Feminine Inquiry*. She lives in East Tennessee, where she teaches at Pellissippi State Community College.

Chang Shih Yen

Chang Shih Yen is a writer from Malaysia. She graduated with first class honours in English and Linguistics, and a MA in Linguistics from the University of Otago in New Zealand. She writes a blog about shoes at https://shihyenshoes.wordpress.com. Six days after she finished writing Letter to my grandmother, Shih Yen's own grandmother passed away. She did not make it home in time to say goodbye.

About The Geeky Press

The Geeky Press is as much a philosophy as it is an entity.

Brad King launched this little group on April 3, 2014, in hopes of building a vibrant writing community in greater downtown Indianapolis. What he didn't have was much of a plan to make that happen. He launched the website, planned a reading series called The Downtown Writers Jam, and hoped that people would come.

And show up they did. Before long, The Geeky Press grew to include more than 100 writers who participated in writing meetups, retreats, reading series, and other literary gatherings.

Before long, The Geeky Press added three amazing partners: Amber Peckham, who is the wittiest writer of the bunch and who corrals our reading series; Nicole Mathew, who has turned our weekly #WritersHack events into a welcoming writing community; and Elise Lockwood, who helps recruit writers to the podcast and runs the Scripted reading series.

While The Geeky Press is generally run by the three of us, we've encouraged participants to create their own writing spaces. Now we have members like Reid Delehanty, who has started hosting his own #WritersHack.

In other words, this labor of love has become everything we'd hoped it would be.

About Brad

Brad earned his Masters of Journalism from the University of California's Graduate School of Journalism in 2000. Worked for *Wired* and *MIT's Technology Review* as a reporter, multimedia editor, senior editor, and producer. Co-authored *Dungeons & Dreamers: A story of how computer games created a global culture.* And serves as a program board member with South by Southwest Interactive.

He's currently the Editor and Director of Carnegie Mellon University's ETC Press, where he's worked in various capacities since 20067. Before that, he was the co-founder and co-director of Ball State University's Center for Emerging Media Design & Development and an associate professor of journalism.

About Amber

The Geeky Press partner Amber Peckham is an amazing talent. She earned her B.A. in Creative Writing from DePauw University in 2009 and her M.F.A. in Creative Nonfiction at Northwestern University in 2014. She's already developing a reading series along with an essay podcast. Plus, she'll join and help host the #WritersHack. She is just generally amazing, we're excited to have her on board.

About Nicole

Nicole graduated with a B.A. in English (Writing & Literacy) from IUPUI in 2010. She went back to IUPUI to earn her Masters to teach English, but life took another turn and she wound up becoming a Project Manager. Between graduation and now, Nicole has been a freelance writer in her spare time, doing a lot of writing for the web. Additionally, she's a coordinating producer for a couple of podcasts. Nicole helps host/organize the #writershack and enjoys connecting with other writers in the Indianapolis area. To learn more about Nicole, visit nicolemathew.com.

About Elise

Elise Lockwood graduated from DePauw University in December 2013 with a B.A. in English Writing. She was awarded the Chad Kostel Memorial Award in Writing and the Barbara Petty Award in Theatre, both from DePauw. Her play *Snatch and Release* will be published in Smith and Krauss, Inc.'s Best Ten-Minute Plays of 2016, coming to shelves this December. In January 2017, her full-length play *Spineless*, will premiere at Bowling Green State University. In real life, Elise completed her graduate student in Ball State University's Emerging Media Design and Development master's program in 2017.

About Vouched Books Indy

Vouched Books Indy is a pop-up bookstore that loves small press literature & Indianapolis. We sell books & we host readings & sometimes we write reviews on our website, vouchedbooks.com, or on Facebook, www.facebook.com/vouchedbooks/.

Jessica Dyer is a writer (of oh so many things) living in Central Indiana. She's an associate editor at *The Arsenic Lobster Poetry Journal* and is the author of the chapbook *Uterus Poems*. She runs Vouched Books Indy (Indianapolis) and is made of star stuff.

Other Publications by The Geeky Press

HoosierLit (Spring 2017)

HoosierLit: A Literary Magazine by The Geeky Press is a publication that features some of the best fiction, non-fiction, essays, poetry, and scriptwriting by Indiana writers. Check out our inaugural Spring issue.

Bad Jobs & Bullshit: It's Unlikely That We Will Be Missed (Vol. 1)

We're just people who have worked a lot of bad jobs, and put up with a lot of bullshit, and decided we wanted to hear about how that same phenomenon happened to others. We think you'll find the mix of essays, short stories, and poems in this collection speak to common experiences and make you feel less alone in your struggle against the grinding machine of entropy.